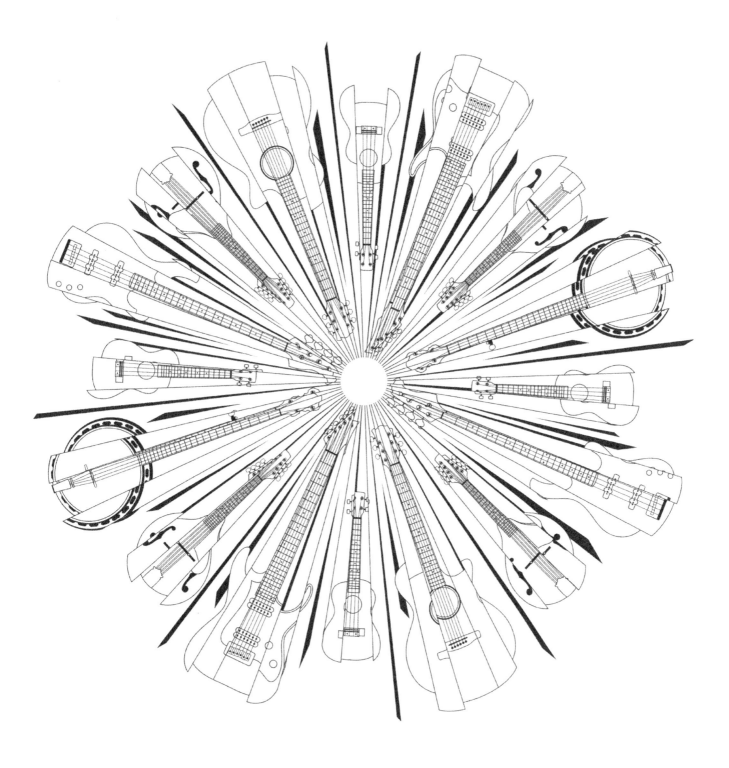

The Ultimate Guitar Chord Book

Here are some of my favourite quotes from respected musicians. Hopefully they inspire you to practice as much as they did me!

'One day you pick up the guitar and you feel like a great master, and the next day you feel like a fool. It's because we're different every day, but the guitar is always the same...beautiful.'

~ Tommy Emmanuel

'Sometimes you want to give up the guitar, you'll hate the guitar. But if you stick with it, you're going to be rewarded.'

~ Jimmy Hendrix

'The beautiful thing about learning is nobody can take it away from you.'

~ B.B. King

'I believe every guitar player inherently has something unique about their playing. They just have to identify what makes them different and develop it.'

~ Jimmy Page

ISBN: 979-8-63615-784-7
www.youtube.com/karlgolden
www.instagram.com/karlgolden
www.facebook.com/karlgoldenguitarist

Contents

Introduction

As with all books in The Ultimate Guitar Series, I wanted to create a bible of useful shapes that will help you unlock the fretboard. With this book we are looking at chord shapes starting from the most basic triad chords to the more advanced extended chords such as ninths, elevenths and thirteenths. So many chord books I have read in the past have hundreds of unnecessary chord shapes that are just repeated in every key. This can be confusing and make players think they have a massive volume of chord shapes to learn, which they don't.

I have found over my 20 years of playing guitar that it is better to learn chord shapes in one key that can then be moved anywhere on the fretboard, which is why I have heavily focused on the CAGED chord shapes in this book. Don't feel like you have to learn them all, learn what you need to help improve your playing. Also, don't worry too much if you do not understand what the CAGED system is, I will give you a basic overview of it in this book. The most important thing to remember is where the root note is, then you can move whatever chord shape you are learning to that position on the fretboard. Easy as pie!

To get the most from this book I highly recommend you learn where each note is on the fretboard, or at the very least on the low strings E, A and D. There is a full chart of every note of the fretboard in this book to help you.

Learning all the notes on the neck will allow you to quickly identify the root note and move the chord shape to that position. Every chord shape in this book will show the root notes with a white circle and you will notice that all the chord shapes are connected over the whole fretboard.

I hope you find this book as useful for your guitar playing as I have in making it and don't forget to check out **www.karlgolden.org/ultimateguitarseries** for free downloads to help you with this book.

All the best,

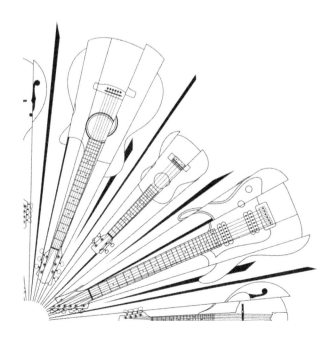

How to Use This Book

For every chord in this book there will be a number of guitar shape boxes, like the one you see below, that represent the fretboard of a guitar and the six strings (standard tuning). These shapes are movable so you will not see any numbers on the frets. With regards to the formula of the chords don't worry if you are not a master of music theory, I have laid out the guitar intervals in the key of D on **page 9**, which are also moveable to whatever key you want and will help you see how these chord shapes have been built. Visit **www.karlgolden.org/ultimateguitarseries** to find recommended hand positions, in the event you are struggling to work out where to put your fingers for the chords.

Below is an example of a Major seventh chord chart that shows you how to read them:

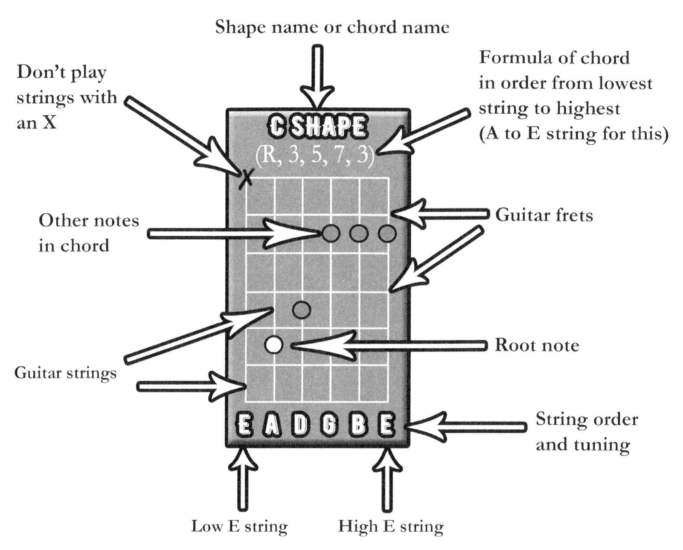

As mentioned in the introduction, I highly recommend you learn all the notes on the fretboard so you can move these chord shapes around; there is a full fretboard diagram on **page 10** that can help you. At first, I suggest learning any notes without sharps or flats on the low E, A and D strings, then you can fill in the gaps later.

Chord Formulas

MAJOR

Symbol Example	Name	Formula
D or Dmaj	Major	1, 3, 5
Dmaj6	Major 6th	1, 3, 5, 6
Dmaj7 or D△7	Major 7th	1, 3, 5, 7
Dmaj9	Major 9th	1, 3, 5, 7, 9
Dmaj11	Major 11th	1, 3, 5, 7, 9, 11
Dmaj13	Major 13th	1, 3, 5, 7, 9, 11, 13
Dmaj6/9	Major 6 9	1, 3, 5, 6, 9
Dmajadd9	Major add 9	1, 3, 5, 9

MINOR

Symbol Example	Name	Formula
Dm or Dmin	Minor	1, ♭3, 5
Dmin6	Minor 6th	1, ♭3, 5, 6
Dmin7	Minor 7th	1, ♭3, 5, ♭7
Dmin9	Minor 9th	1, ♭3, 5, ♭7, 9
Dmin11	Minor 11th	1, ♭3, 5, ♭7, 9, 11
Dmin13	Minor 13th	1, ♭3, 5, ♭7, 9, 11, 13
Dmin6/9	Minor 6 9	1, ♭3, 5, 6, 9
Dminadd9	Minor add 9	1, ♭3, 5, 9

DOMINANT

Symbol Example	Name	Formula
D7	Dominant 7th	1, 3, 5, ♭7
D7/6	Dominant 7 6	1, 3, 5, 6, ♭7
D7/11	Dominant 7 11	1, 3, 5, ♭7, 11
D9	Dominant 9th	1, 3, 5, ♭7, 9
D11	Dominant 11th	1, 3, 5, ♭7, 9, 11
D13	Dominant 13th	1, 3, 5, ♭7, 9, 11, 13
D9sus4	Dominant 9 Sus 4	1, 4, 5, ♭7, 9
D7#11	Dominant sharp 11	1, 3, 5, ♭7, #11
D13sus4	Dominant 13 sus 4	1, 4, 5, ♭7, 9, 11, 13

SUSPENDED

Symbol Example	Name	Formula
Dsus2	Suspended 2nd	1, 2, 5
Dsus4	Suspended 4th	1, 4, 5
D7sus2	7th Sus 2	1, 2, 5, ♭7
D7sus4	7th Sus 4	1, 4, 5, ♭7

DIMINISHED

Symbol Example	Name	Formula
Dmin7♭5 or Dø	Half-Diminished	1, ♭3, ♭5, ♭7
Ddim7 or D°	Fully-Diminished	1, ♭3, ♭5, ♭♭7

ALTERED CHORDS

Symbol Example	Name	Formula
D7♭5	Dominant Flat 5	1, 3, ♭5, ♭7
D7#5 or D7+5	Dominant Sharp 5	1, 3, #5, ♭7
D7#9 or D7+9	Dominant Sharp 9	1, 3, 5, ♭7, #9
D7♭9	Dominant Flat 9	1, 3, 5, ♭7, ♭9
D7#5♭9	Dominant Sharp 5 Flat 9	1, 3, #5, ♭7, ♭9
D7♭5#9	Dominant Flat 5 Sharp 9	1, 3, ♭5, ♭7, #9

OTHER

Example	Name	Formula
Dmin(maj)7	Minor Major 7th	1, ♭3, 5, 7
Daug or D+	Augmented	1, 3, #5
D5	Power Chords	1, 5

Don't worry if you don't really understand the theory of chords and the way they are built, it won't affect you learning all the shapes in this book. It's more important you experiment with new chords and apply them to your song-writing or every day playing, helping you to spice up your average major or minor chords.

Hopefully as you work your way through this book you will find yourself understanding how chords evolve from their simplest forms. I always say in my books that none of this is rocket science, it's all maths and once you break the code you will be flying!

Guitar Intervals in the Key Of D

Here are all the intervals on the fretboard in the key of D (all the audio and picture examples of hand positions on my website are using the key of D). You can use this to visualize how the chord shapes are formed with the formulas. There is a total of twelve notes on the fretboard that just repeat in octaves over the different strings (based on standard tuning).

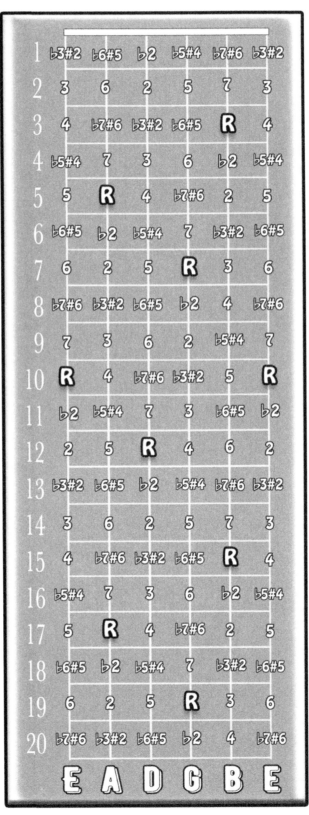

Notes on the Fretboard

Here are all the notes on the fretboard with standard tuning. It is worth spending some time to learn these as it will help you move the chord shapes given in this book to any key you desire. Notice that the high and low E strings have exactly the same note order but two octaves apart, so there are only another four strings to learn after that!

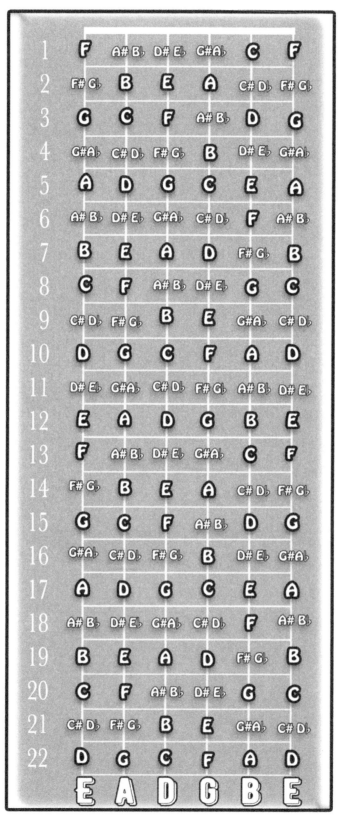

Triads

A chord is defined as being three notes or more which makes the triad the most basic form of a chord. The term triad refers to a chord with three notes stacked in thirds with a root, third and fifth. The main and most useful triads are the major (R, 3, 5), minor, (R, ♭3, 5), diminished (R, ♭3, ♭5) and augmented (R, 3, #5). This book will also take a look at some suspended triads known as sus chords (or suspended chords), such as the sus two (R, 2, 5) and sus four (R, 4, 5). With suspended chords and triads, the third is always omitted and it is then neither a major or minor chord.

There are three different ways to arrange triads on the guitar. Here is an example using D major triads;

ROOT POSITION (R, 3, 5) **1ˢᵀ INVERSION (3, 5, R)** **2ⁿᵈ INVERSION (5, R, 3)**

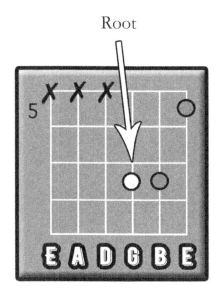
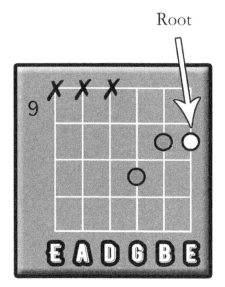
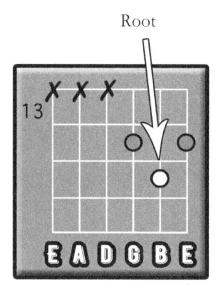

Root Position – The root note is in the bass or lower note.
1ˢᵗ Inversion – The third is in the bass or lower note.
2ⁿᵈ Inversion – The fifth is in the bass or lower note.

This book will go through the twelve essential shapes you should learn with the three different inversions on each set of the three string combinations on a standard six string guitar for all the triads. Learning these triad shapes all over the fretboard will be extremely beneficial to build an understanding of how chords are built from their simplest form, but not only that they can be very useful in improvising, song-writing and building other chord shapes. You will be amazed how playing a simple triad in a different inversion can change the vibe of a chord progression, as well as being useful in improvisation situations to help outline and find other relating chords, scales and arpeggios.

Major Triads
Formula (R, 3, 5)

Major triads are built from the root, major third, and perfect fifth. As explained in the previous chapter, there are three different arrangements of the notes which are: root position, 1st inversion, and 2nd inversion. In the root position the root note will be in the bass, in the 1st inversion position the major third will be in the bass, and finally in the 2nd inversion the fifth will be in the bass, covering all the different combinations.

I have arranged the shapes below starting from the low strings E, A and D moving up to the high strings G, B and E. I highly recommend you learn these shapes inside out, practising up and down the fretboard. These shapes are a valuable tool not only in understanding how chords are built but helping you improvise, connect scales, and build arpeggios.

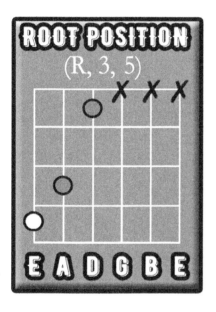

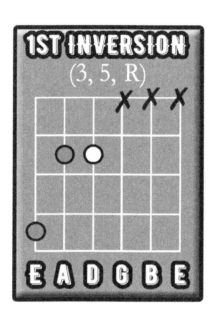

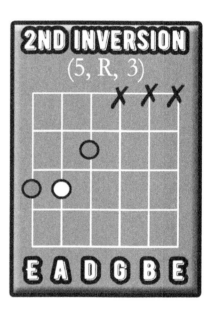

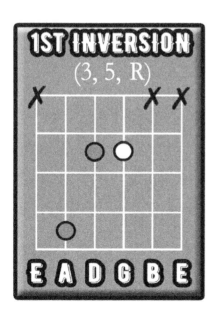

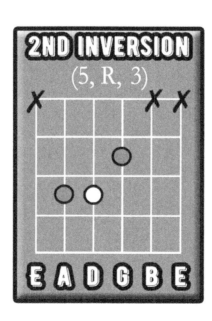

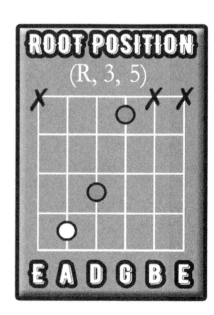

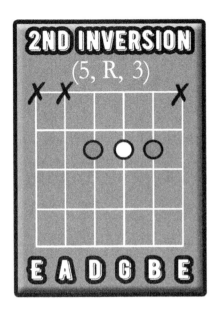 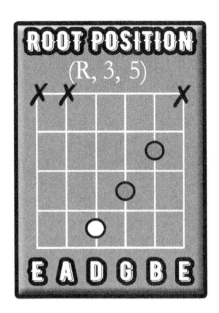 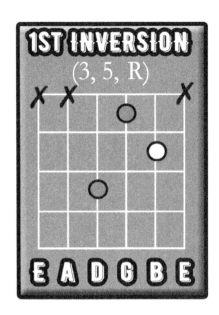

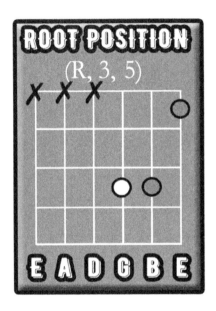 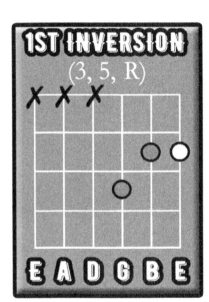 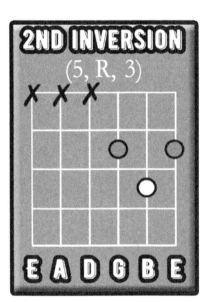

Improvising Over Major Triads

You can use the major scale, also known as Ionian mode, the major pentatonic, and any major arpeggios to improvise over major triads. For example, if you are playing a D major triad in a song, any notes from the D major scale or a D major seventh arpeggio will sound great. There is a lot more flexibility with scales and arpeggios when the chord you are playing over has only a few intervals. You can imply other flavours on top with your solo note choice.

Some other modes to explore that work well are Lydian, Mixolydian, Lydian sharp two, Lydian flat seven and Mixolydian flat six.

Make sure you check out my other books in this series if you want to learn more about different scales, arpeggios, and shapes that are mentioned in this book.

Practising Major Triads

As well as the obvious strumming and playing these chords up and down the neck, here are some fun picking exercises to help you remember the shapes. In **Exercise 1** below, use alternate picking through every inversion shape horizontally on each of the three string combinations, starting with the root inversion for each string grouping in the key of D. I recommend practising in all twelve keys - using the circle of fifths is a great way of organising a way to play in every key **(See page 79).**

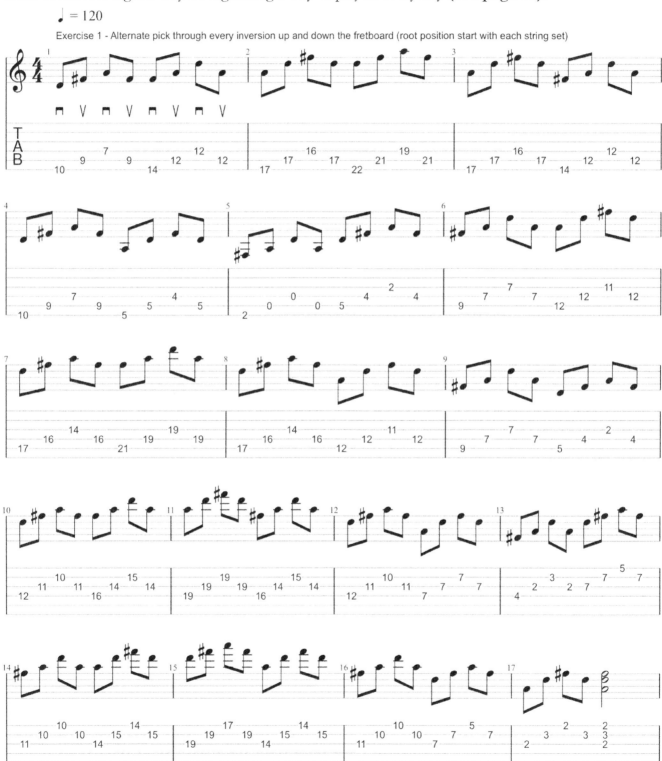

14

Next time you practice try starting **Exercise 1** from the 1st inversion instead of the root and then finally from the 2nd inversion. This will really test to see if you know the shapes inside out.

Exercise 2 is a great way to practice connecting the three different shapes vertically over the strings. This example starts from the root position on the G, B and E strings. Similar to **Exercise 1**, you are arpeggiating the chord which helps you familiarise yourself with the individual notes within that chord.

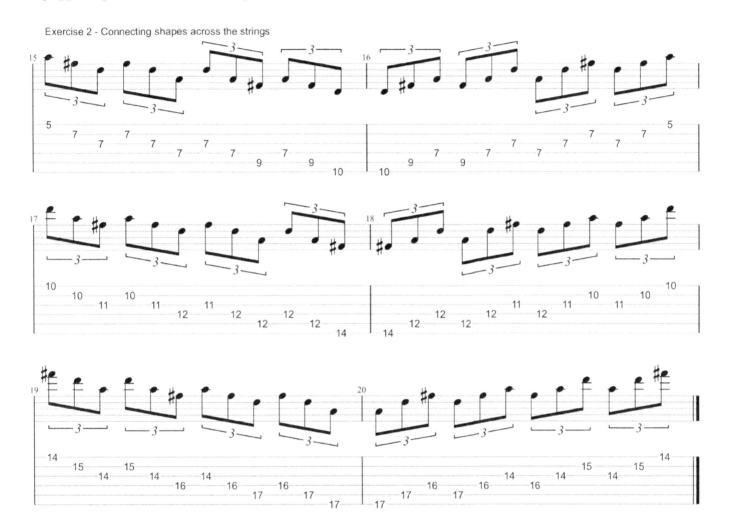

Exercise 2 - Connecting shapes across the strings

Visit **www.karlgolden.org/ultimateguitarseries** to download audio of all the exercises in this book.

Minor Triads

Formula (R, ♭3, 5)

Minor triads are built from the root, minor/flat third, and perfect fifth. In the root position the root note will be in the bass, in the 1st inversion position the minor third will be in the bass, and finally in the 2nd inversion the fifth will be in the bass, covering all the different combinations. As with all triads on a standard six string guitar, there are twelve essential shapes you should learn with the three different inversions on each set of three strings.

I have arranged the shapes below starting from the low strings E, A and D moving up to the high strings G, B and E. I highly recommend you learn these shapes inside out, practising up and down the fretboard.

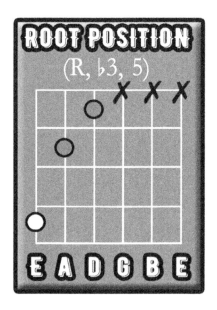

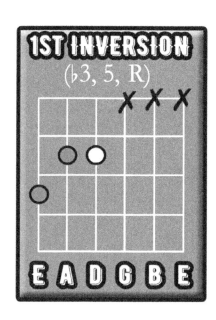

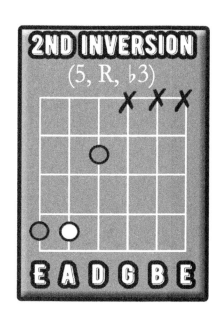

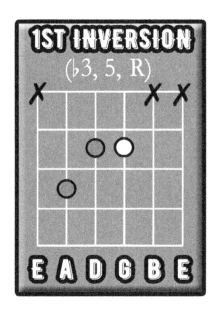

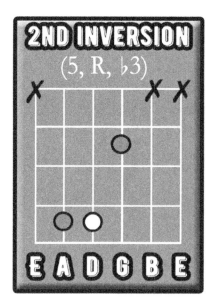

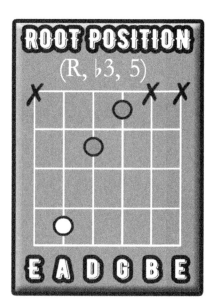

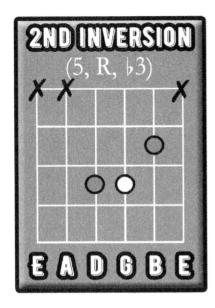

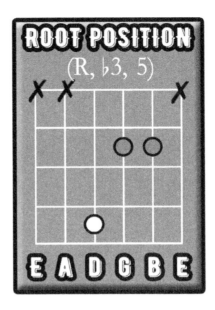

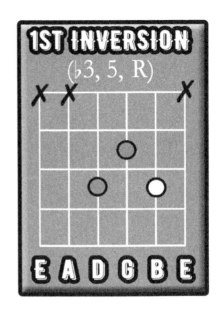

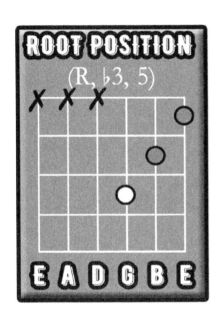

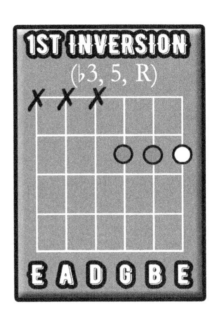

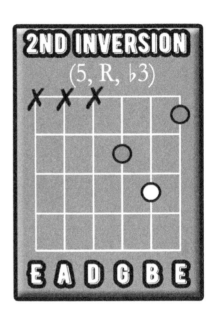

Improvising Over Minor Triads

You can use the natural minor scale, also known as Aeolian mode, the minor pentatonic, the blues scale, and any minor arpeggios to improvise over minor triads. For example, if you are playing a D minor triad in a song, any notes from the D Aeolian mode or a D minor 7 arpeggio will sound great. There is a lot more flexibility with scales and arpeggios when the chord you are playing over has only a few intervals. You can imply other flavours on top with your solo note choice.

Some other modes to explore that work well are; Harmonic minor, Dorian, Phrygian, Dorian sharp four, Phrygian Dominant and Dorian flat two.

17

Practising Minor Triads

Same with the major triads in the previous section, in **Exercise 3** below, use alternate picking through every inversion shape horizontally on each of the three string combinations, starting with the root inversion for each string grouping in the key of D. I recommend practising in all twelve keys - using the circle of fifths is a great way of organising a way to play in every key.

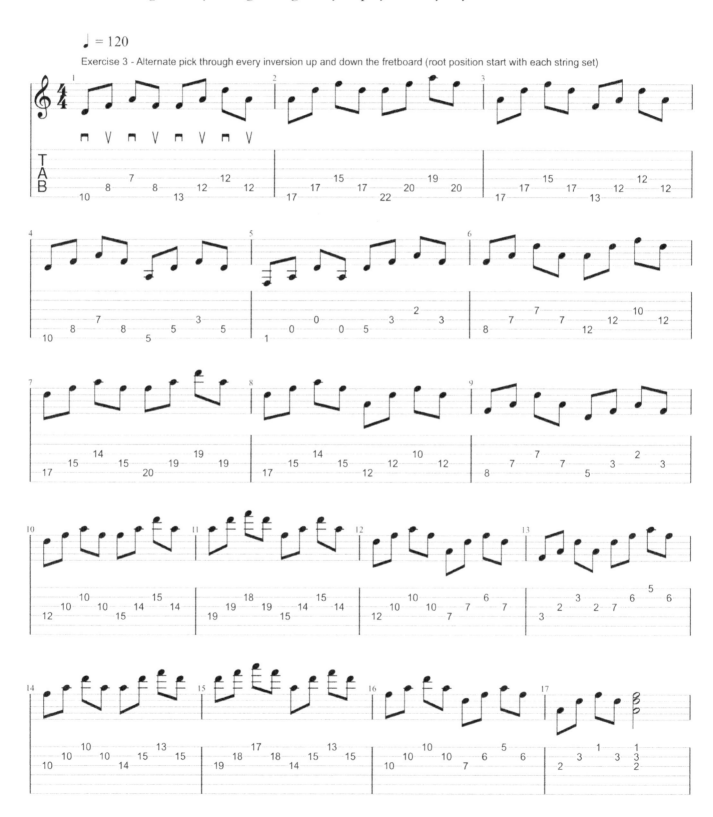

Next time you practice try starting **Exercise 3** from the 1st inversion instead of the root and then finally from the 2nd inversion. This will really test to see if you know the shapes inside out.

Exercise 4 is a great way to practice connecting the three different shapes vertically over strings. This example starts from the root position on the G, B and E strings. Similar to **Exercise 3**, you are arpeggiating the chord which helps you familiarise yourself with the individual notes within that chord.

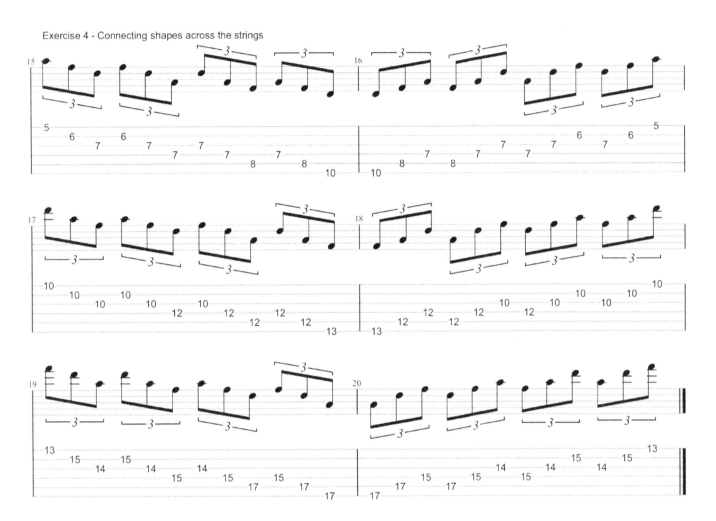

Exercise 4 - Connecting shapes across the strings

Diminished Triads
Formula (R, ♭3, ♭5)

Diminished triads are built from the root, minor/flat third, and diminished/flat fifth. In the root position the root note will be in the bass, in the 1st inversion position the minor third will be in the bass, and finally in the 2nd inversion the diminished fifth will be in the bass, covering all the different combinations. As with all triads on a standard six string guitar there are twelve essential shapes you should learn with the three different inversions on each set of three strings.

I have arranged the shapes below starting from the low strings E, A and D moving up to the high strings G, B and E. I highly recommend you learn these shapes inside out, practising up and down the fretboard.

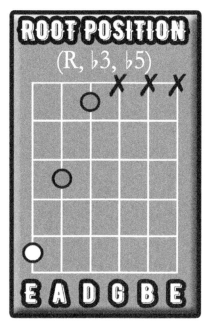

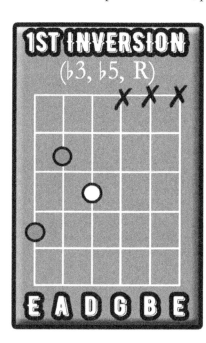

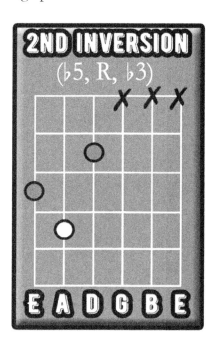

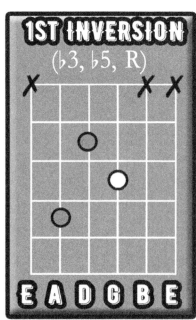

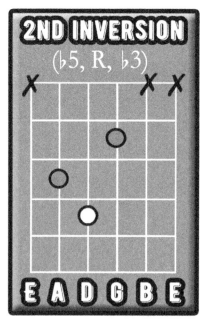

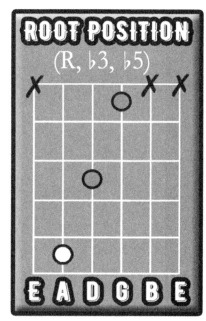

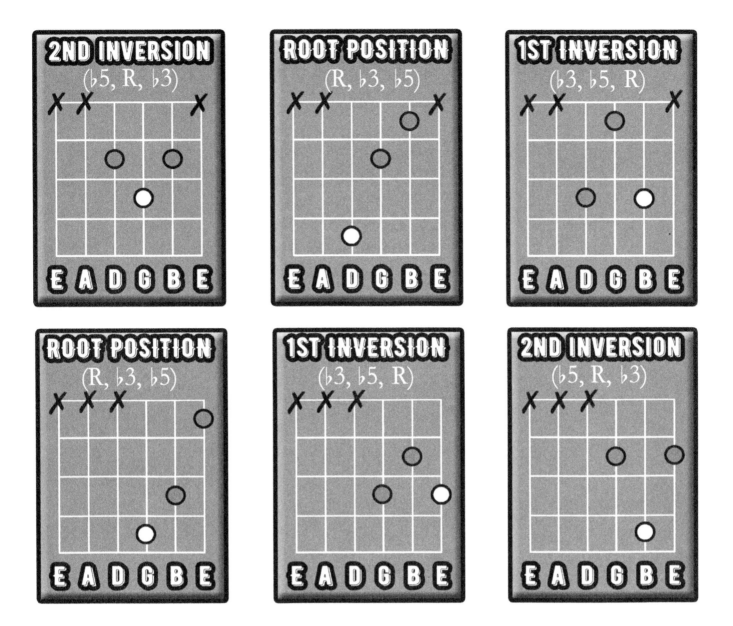

Improvising Over Diminished Triads

You can use the half whole diminished scale and diminished arpeggios to improvise over diminished triads. For example, if you are playing a D diminished triad in a song, any notes from the D half whole diminished scale or a D diminished 7 arpeggio will sound great. There is a lot more flexibility with scales and arpeggios when the chord you are playing over has only a few intervals. You can imply other flavours on top with your solo note choice.

Some other modes to explore that work well are; Locrian, Locrian Natural 6, Super Locrian and Altered scale.

Practising Diminished Triads

As with the previous sections, **Exercise 5** below, uses alternate picking through every inversion shape horizontally on each of the three string combinations, starting with the root inversion for each string grouping in the key of D. Again, I recommend practising in all twelve keys and using the circle of fifths is a great way of organising a way to play in every key.

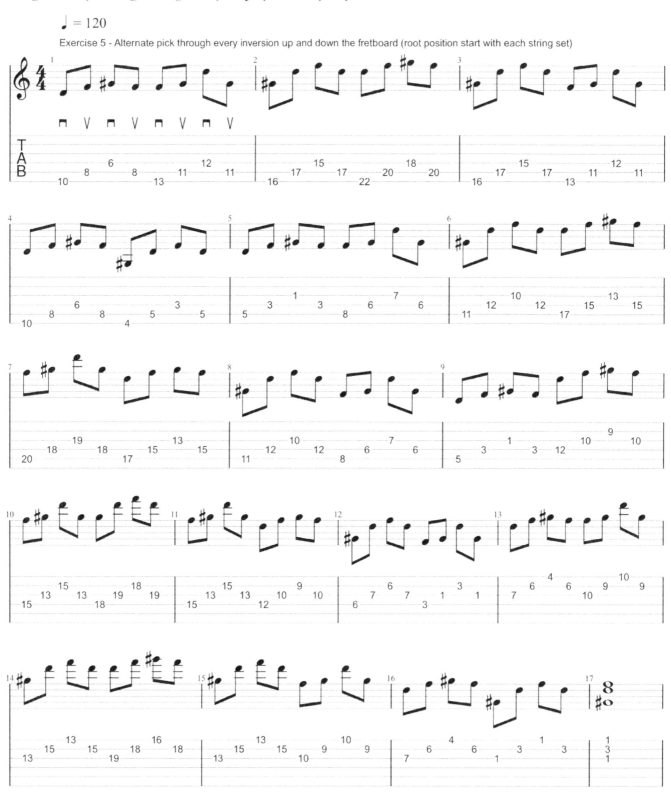

Next time you practice try starting **Exercise 5** from the 1st inversion instead of the root and then finally from the 2nd inversion. This will really test to see if you know the shapes inside out.

Exercise 6 is a great way to practice connecting the three different shapes vertically over strings. This example starts from the root position on the G, B and E strings. Similar to **Exercise 5**, you are arpeggiating the chord which helps you familiarise yourself with the individual notes within that chord.

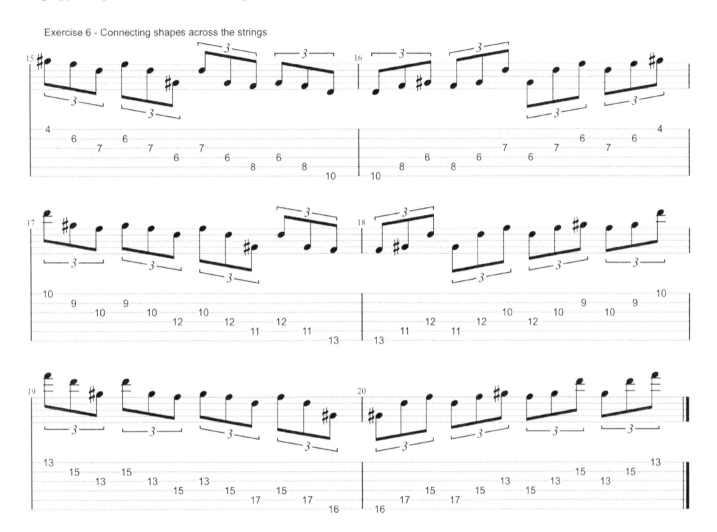

Exercise 6 - Connecting shapes across the strings

Augmented Triads

Formula (R, 3, #5)

Augmented triads are built from the root, major third, and augmented/sharp fifth. In the root position the root note will be in the bass, in the 1st inversion position the major third will be in the bass, and finally in the 2nd inversion the augmented fifth will be in the bass, covering all the different combinations. As with all triads on a standard six string guitar there are twelve essential shapes you should learn with the three different inversions on each set of three strings.

I have arranged the shapes below starting from the low strings E, A and D moving up to the high strings G, B and E. I highly recommend you learn these shapes inside out, practising up and down the fretboard.

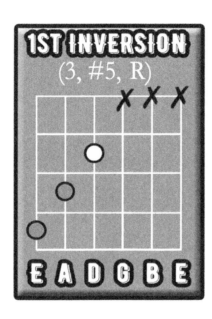

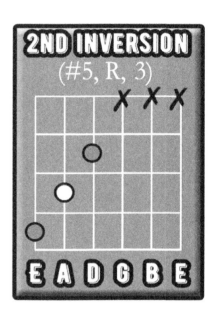

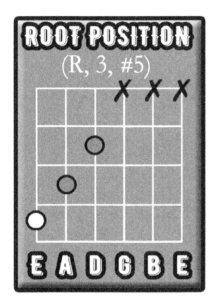

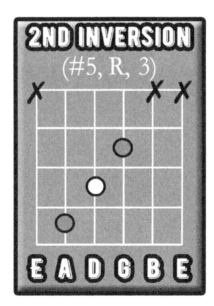

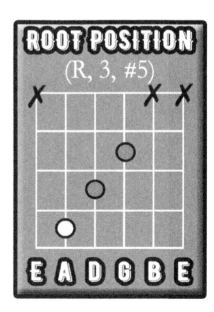

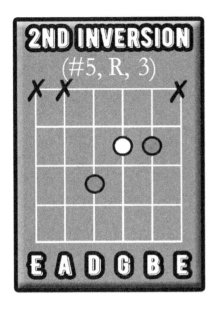

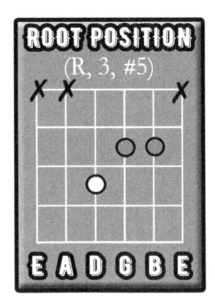

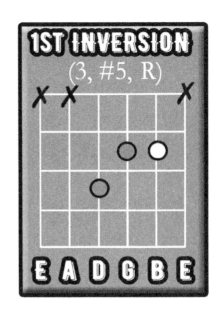

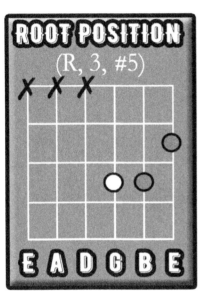

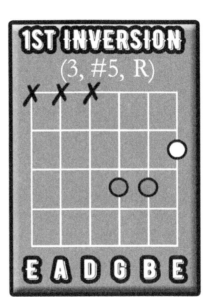

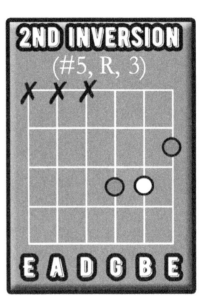

Improvising Over Augmented Triads

You can use the augmented scale and augmented arpeggios to improvise over augmented triads. For example, if you are playing a D augmented triad in a song, any notes from the D augmented scale or a D augmented 7 arpeggio will sound great. There is a lot more flexibility with scales and arpeggios when the chord you are playing over has only a few intervals. You can imply other flavours on top with your solo note choice.

Some other modes to explore that work well are; Lydian augmented and Ionian sharp five.

Practising Augmented Triads

In the same way as the previous sections, **Exercise 7** alternate picks through every inversion shape horizontally on each of the three string combinations, starting with the root inversion for each string grouping in the key of D. As mentioned previously, the circle of fifths is a great way of organising a way to play in every key.

♩ = 120

Exercise 7 - Alternate pick through every inversion up and down the fretboard (root position start with each string set)

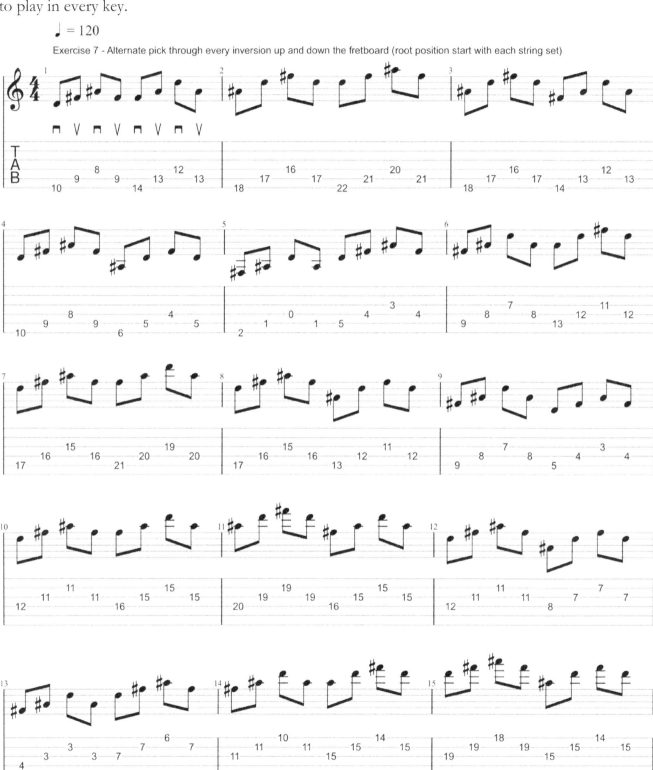

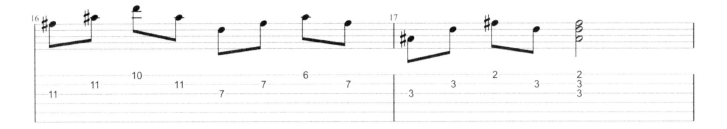

Next time you practice try starting **Exercise 7** from the 1st inversion instead of the root and then finally from the 2nd inversion. This will really test to see if you know the shapes inside out.

Exercise 8 is a great way to practice connecting the three different shapes vertically over strings. This example starts from the root position on the G, B and E strings. Similar to **Exercise 7**, you are arpeggiating the chord which helps you familiarise yourself with the individual notes within that chord.

Exercise 8 - Connecting shapes across the strings

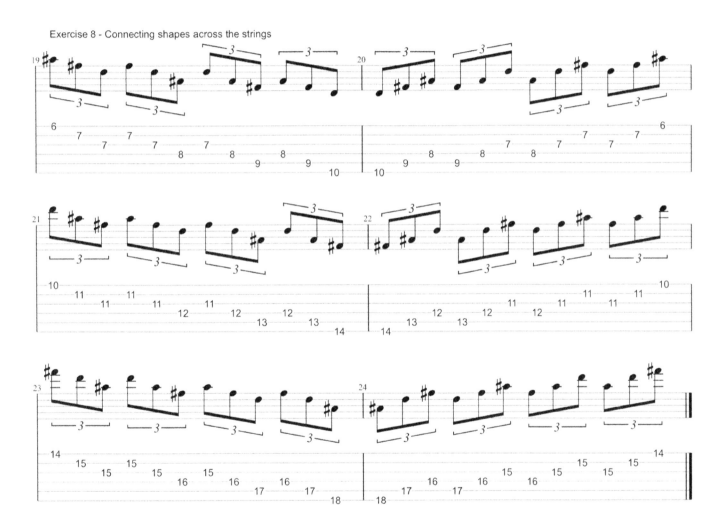

Sus Two Triads
Formula (R, 2, 5)

Suspended, or sus two triads are built from the root, major second, and perfect fifth. In the root position the root note will be in the bass, in the 1st inversion position the major second will be in the bass, and finally in the 2nd inversion the fifth will be in the bass, covering all the different combinations. As with all triads on a standard six string guitar there are twelve essential shapes you should learn with the three different inversions on each set of three strings.

I have arranged the shapes below starting from the low strings E, A and D moving up to the high strings G, B and E. I highly recommend you learn these shapes inside out, practising up and down the fretboard.

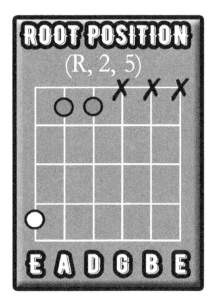
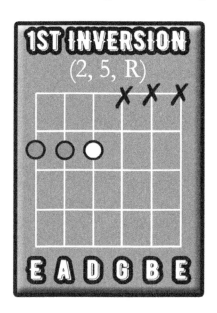
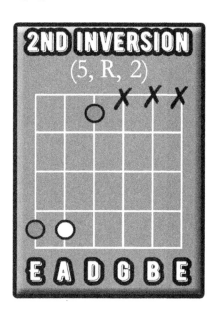

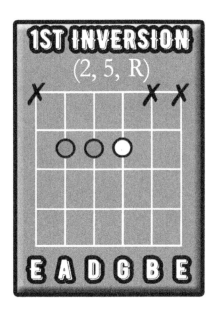
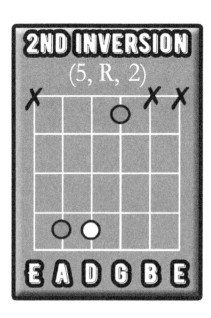
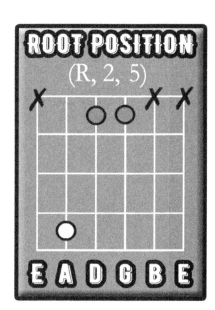

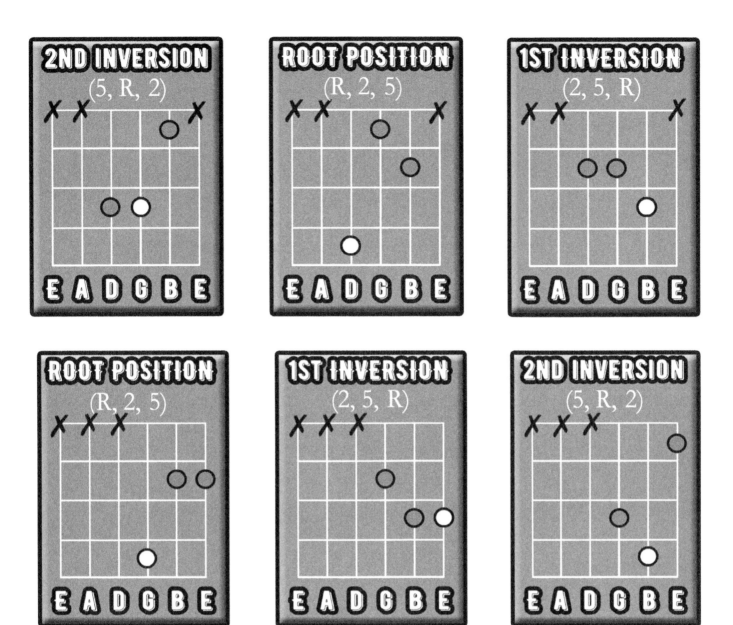

Improvising Over Sus 2 Triads

Since there is no third in suspended triads you can play a range of major, minor scales and modes that work well. It gets more restricted when you harmonise to the 7th degree and upwards as you are adding more notes to the chord. The Mixolydian and Lydian modes are a great start to experiment with.

Practising Sus Two Triads

Exercise 9 below uses alternate picking through every inversion shape horizontally on each of the three string combinations, starting with the root inversion for each string grouping in the key of D. I recommend practising in all twelve keys.

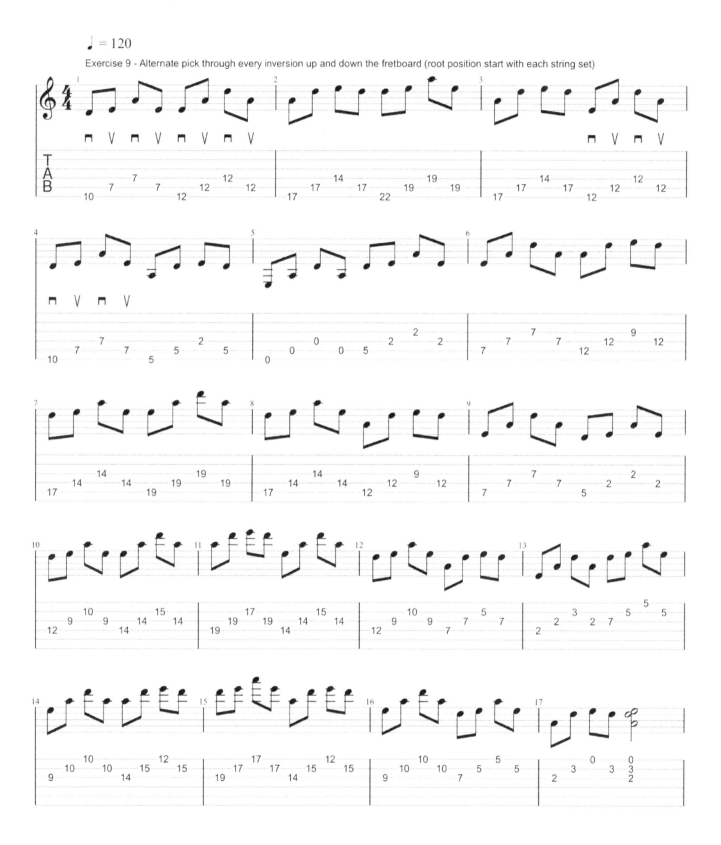

Next time you practice try starting **Exercise 9** from the 1st inversion instead of the root and then finally from the 2nd inversion. This will really test to see if you know the shapes inside out.

Exercise 10 is a great way to practice connecting the three different shapes vertically over strings. This example starts from the root position on the G, B and E strings. Similar to **Exercise 9**, you are arpeggiating the chord which helps you familiarise yourself with the individual notes within that chord.

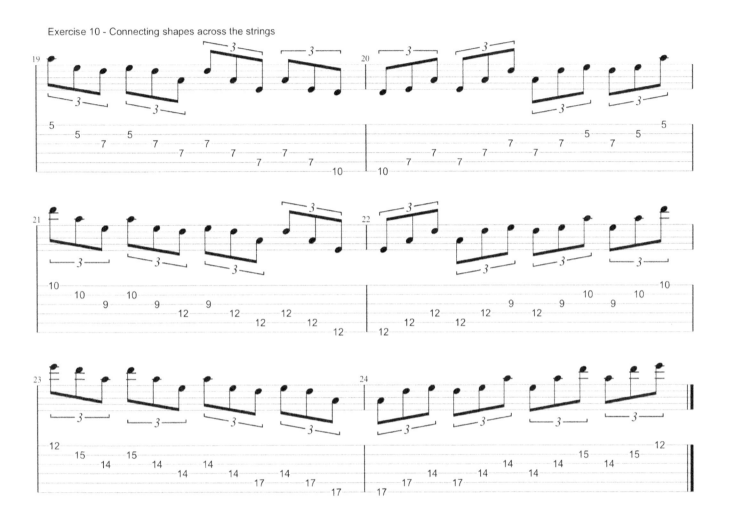

Exercise 10 - Connecting shapes across the strings

Sus Four Triads
Formula (R, 4, 5)

Suspended, or sus, four triads are built from the root, perfect fourth, and perfect fifth. In the root position the root note will be in the bass, in the 1st inversion position the fourth will be in the bass, and finally in the 2nd inversion the fifth will be in the bass, covering all the different combinations. As with all triads on a standard six string guitar, there are twelve essential shapes you should learn with the three different inversions on each set of three strings.

I have arranged the shapes below starting from the low strings E, A and D moving up to the high strings G, B and E. I highly recommend you learn these shapes inside out, practising up and down the fretboard.

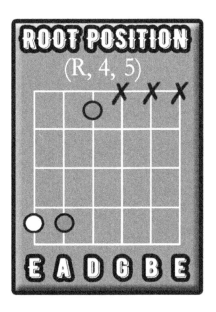

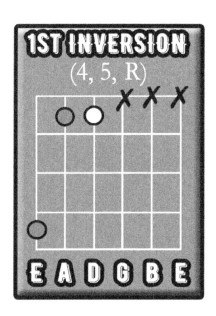

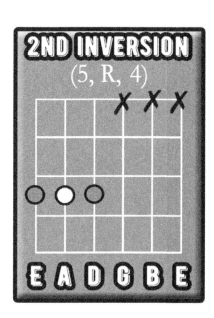

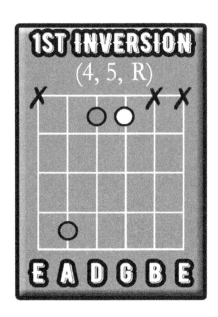

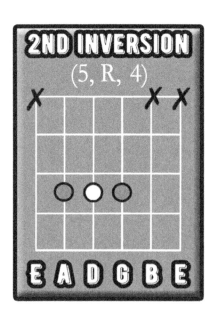

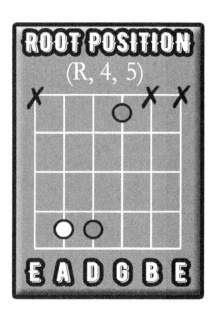

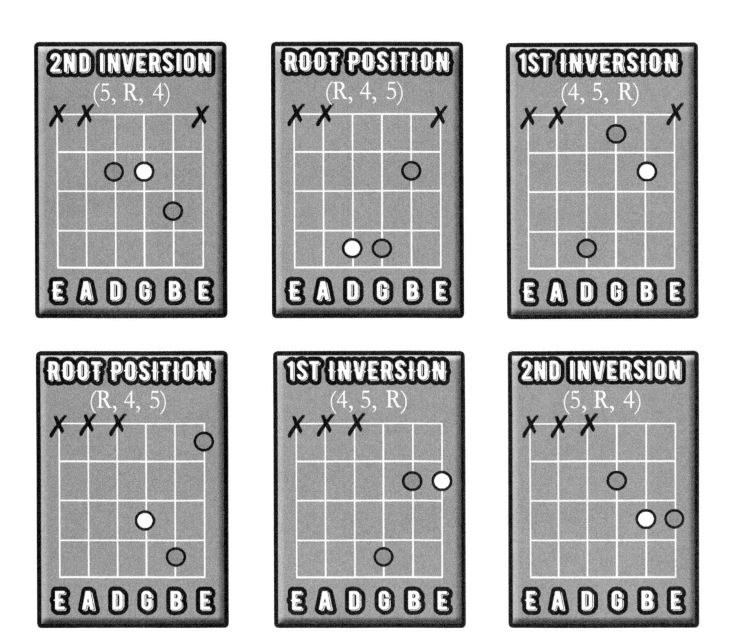

Improvising Over Sus 4 Triads

Like sus 2 chords, since there is no third in suspended triads you can play a range of major and minor scales and modes that work well. It gets more restricted when you harmonise to the 7th degree and upwards as you are adding more notes to the chord. The Mixolydian and Lydian modes are a great start to experiment with.

Practising Sus Four Triads

As with previous sections, in **Exercise 11** below uses alternate picking through every inversion shape horizontally on each of the three string combinations, starting with the root inversion for each string grouping in the key of D. As always I recommend practising these in all twelve keys.

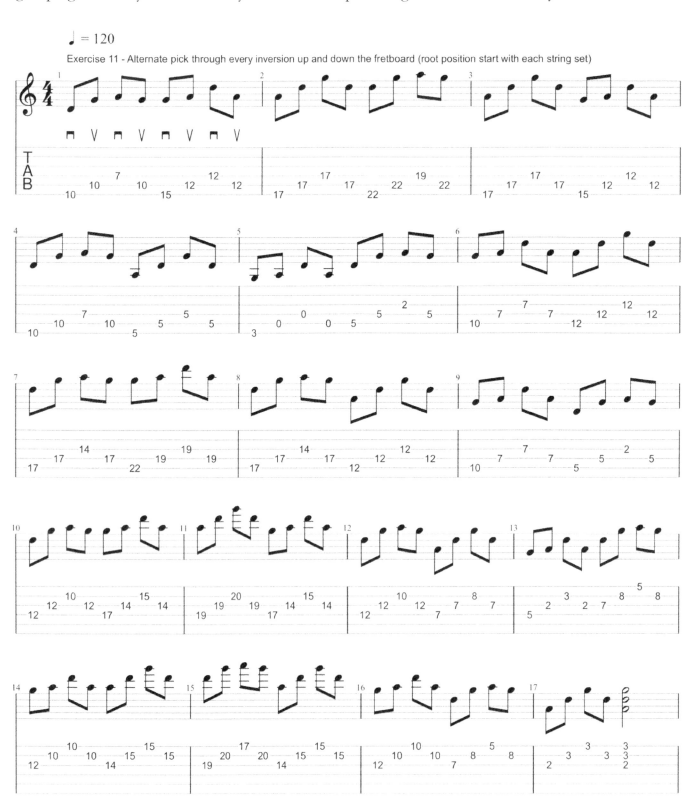

34

Next time you practice try starting **Exercise 11** from the 1st inversion instead of the root and then finally from the 2nd inversion. This will really test to see if you know the shapes inside out.

Exercise 12 is a great way to practice connecting the three different shapes vertically over strings. This example starts from the root position on the G, B and E strings. Similar to **Exercise 11**, you are arpeggiating the chord which helps you familiarise yourself with the individual notes within that chord.

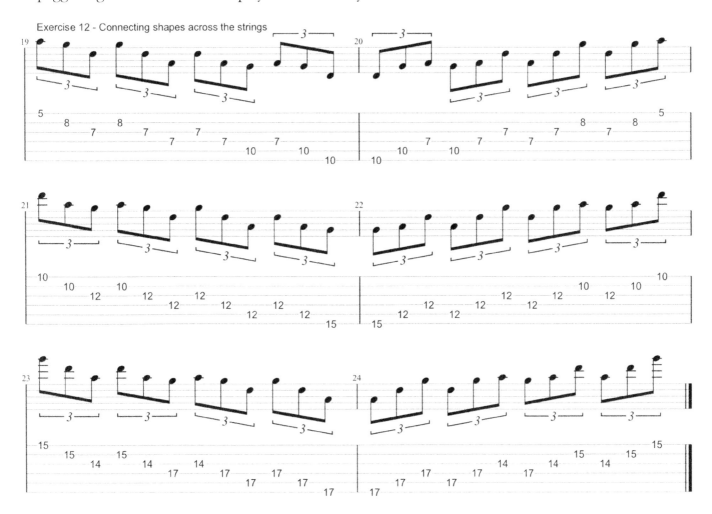

Exercise 12 - Connecting shapes across the strings

Major Chords
Formula (R, 3, 5)

Basic major chords are formed with the root, major third and perfect fifth. Using the CAGED system **(see page 77)**, below are five moveable shapes that allow you to play the same major chord all over the fretboard. Don't worry if you don't understand how the CAGED system works, it is more important that you understand that by using the root note you can move these shapes to any key you want on the fretboard. Visit **www.karlgolden.org/ultimateguitarseries** for pictures of recommended hand positions on the fretboard. The major scale (Ionian mode) and major pentatonic sound great over these chords for improvisation.

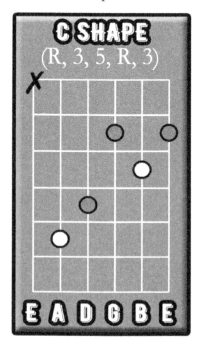

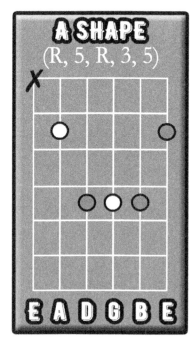

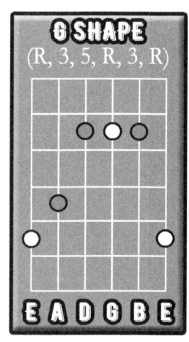

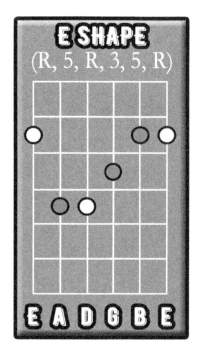

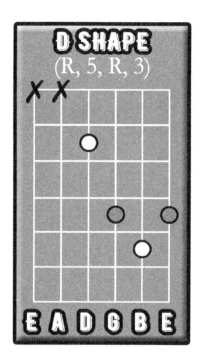

36

Minor Chords
Formula (R, ♭3, 5)

Basic minor chords are formed with the root, minor third and perfect fifth. Using the CAGED system, below are five moveable shapes that allow you to play the same minor chord all over the fretboard. The natural minor scale (Aeolian mode), minor pentatonic, blues scale, and Dorian mode sound great for improvisation over these chords.

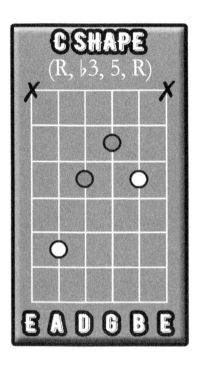

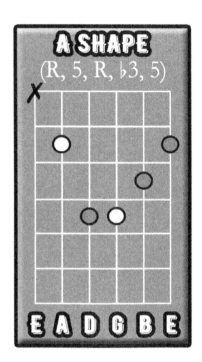

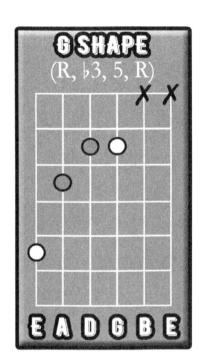

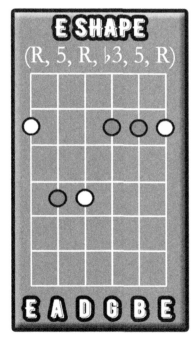

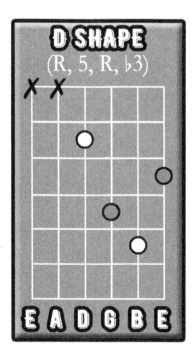

Diminished Chords
Formula (R, ♭3, ♭5)

Basic diminished chords are formed with the root, minor third and diminished/flat fifth. Using the CAGED system, below are five moveable shapes that allow you to play the same diminished chord all over the fretboard. The diminished scales work well over this chord for improvisation.

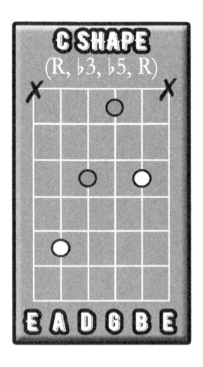

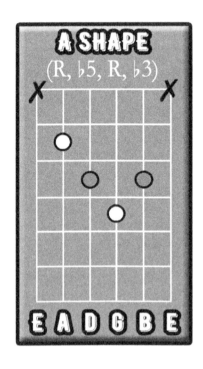

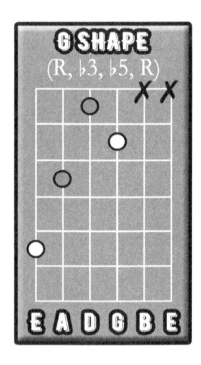

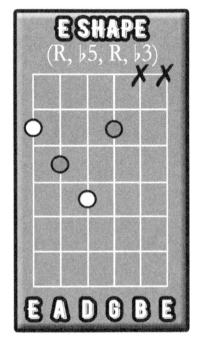

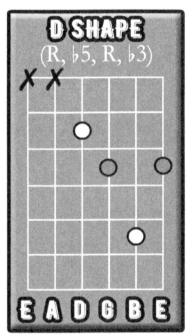

Augmented Chords
Formula (R, 3, #5)

Basic augmented chords are formed with the root, minor third and augmented/sharp fifth. Using the CAGED system, below are five moveable shapes that allow you to play the same augmented chord all over the fretboard. Ionian sharp five mode sounds great for improvising over this chord.

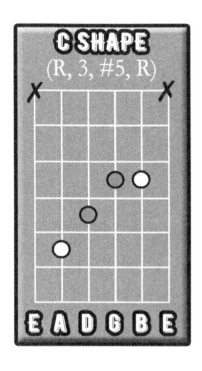

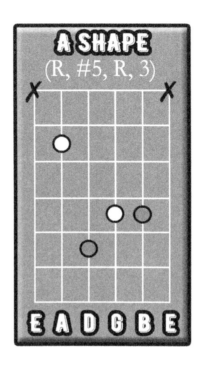

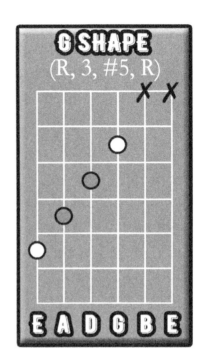

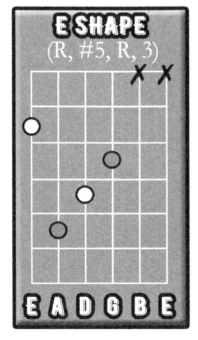

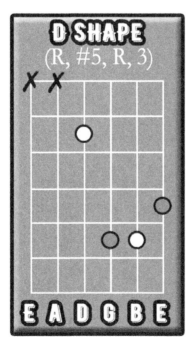

Sus Two Chords
Formula (R, 2, 5)

Suspended or sus two chords are formed with the root, major second and perfect fifth. The third is replaced with the major second so it can't be classed as a major or a minor chord. Using the CAGED system, below are five moveable shapes that allow you to play the same sus two chord all over the fretboard. Lydian and Mixolydian mode sound great for improvisation over these chords.

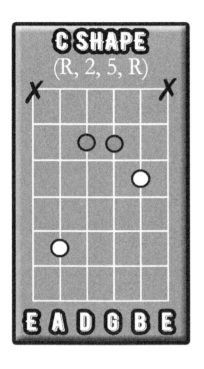

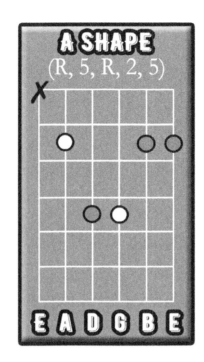

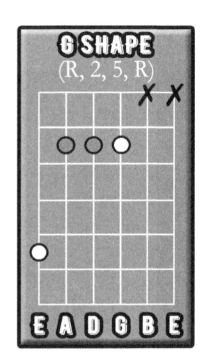

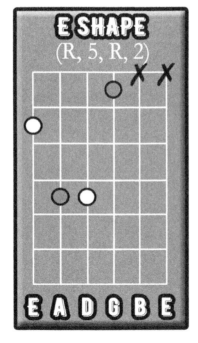

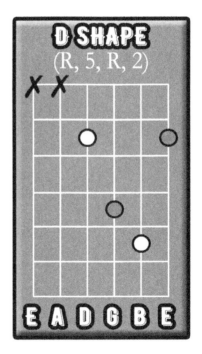

Sus Four Chords
Formula (R, 4, 5)

Sus four chords are formed with the root, perfect fourth and perfect fifth. The third is replaced with the fourth so it can't be classed as a major or a minor chord. Using the CAGED system below, are five moveable shapes that allow you to play the same sus four chord all over the fretboard. Lydian and Mixolydian mode sound great for improvisation over these chords but many more scales will work with the missing minor third so experiment with some minor and major scales.

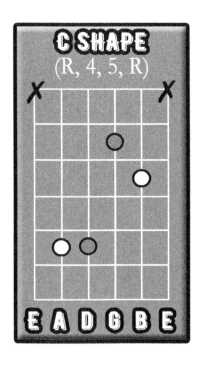

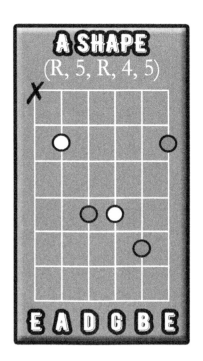

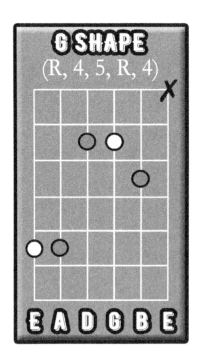

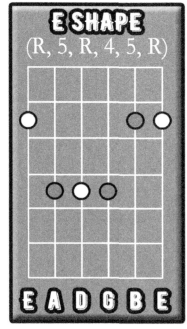

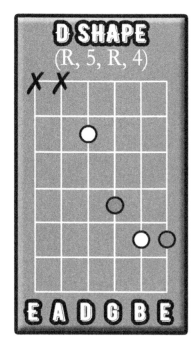

Major Sixth Chords
Formula (R, 3, 5, 6)

Major sixth chords are formed with the root, major third, perfect fifth and major sixth. Using the CAGED system, below are five moveable shapes that allow you to play the same major sixth chord all over the fretboard. The major scale (Ionian mode) and major pentatonic sound great over these chords for improvisation.

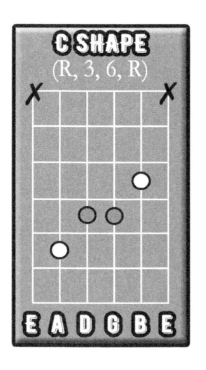

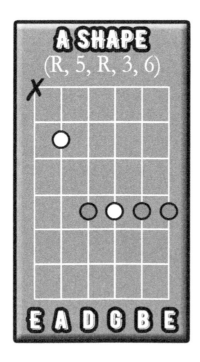

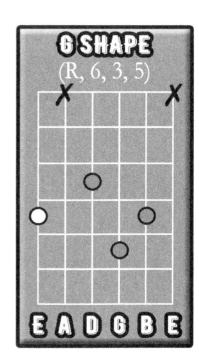

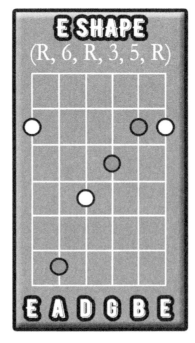

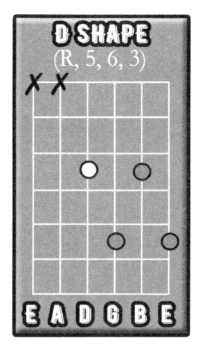

Minor Sixth Chords

Formula (R, ♭3, 5, 6)

Minor sixth chords are formed with the root, minor third, perfect fifth and major sixth. Using the CAGED system, below are five moveable shapes that allow you to play the same minor sixth chord all over the fretboard. The natural minor scale (Aeolian mode), minor pentatonic, blues scale and Dorian mode sound great for improvisation over these chords.

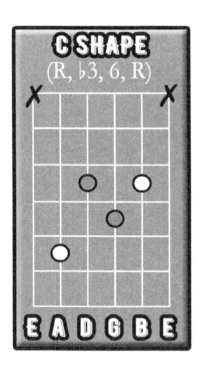

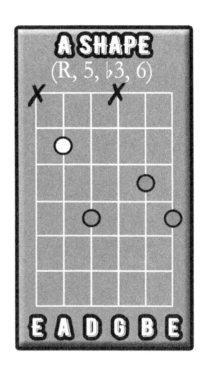

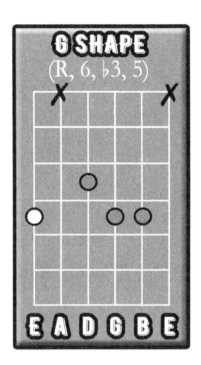

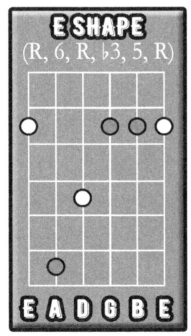

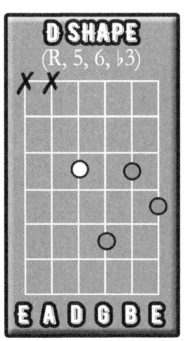

Major Seven Chords
Formula (R, 3, 5, 7)

Major seventh chords are formed with the root, major third, perfect fifth and major seventh. Using the CAGED system, below are five moveable shapes that allow you to play the same major seventh chord all over the fretboard. The major scale (Ionian mode) and major pentatonic sound great over these chords for improvisation.

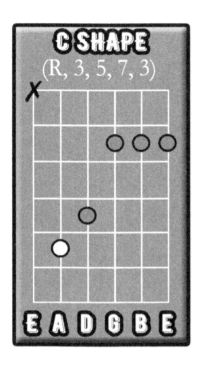

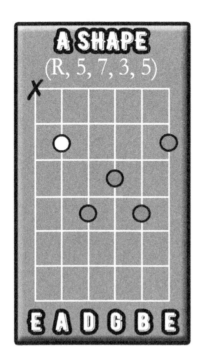

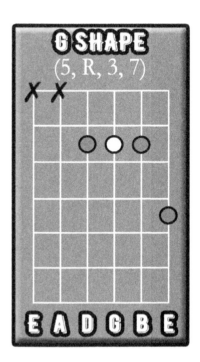

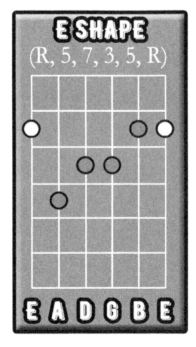

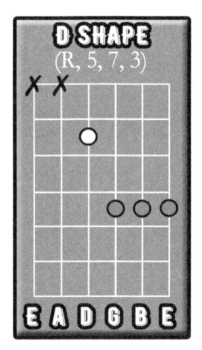

Minor Seven Chords

Formula (R, ♭3, 5, ♭7)

Minor seventh chords are formed with the root, minor third, perfect fifth and minor seventh. Using the CAGED system, below are five moveable shapes that allow you to play the same minor seventh chord all over the fretboard. The natural minor scale (Aeolian mode), minor pentatonic, blues scale and Dorian mode sound great for improvisation over these chords.

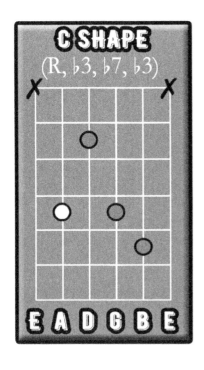

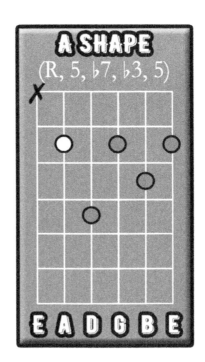

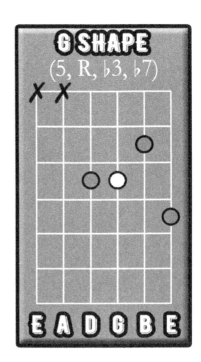

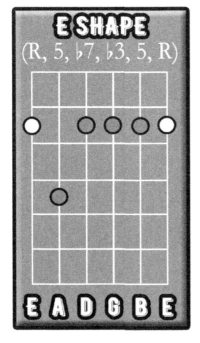

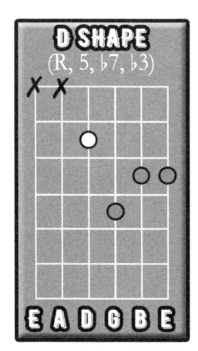

Dominant Seven Chords
Formula (R, 3, 5, ♭7)

Dominant seventh chords are formed with the root, major third, perfect fifth and minor seventh. Using the CAGED system, below are five moveable shapes that allow you to play the same dominant seventh chord all over the fretboard. Probably one of the most versatile chords to improvise over, with major pentatonic, Mixolydian mode, Lydian flat 7 mode, Phrygian Dominant mode, Mixolydian flat six, half/whole diminished, whole tone scale and Super Locrian mode working well over the top of the chord.

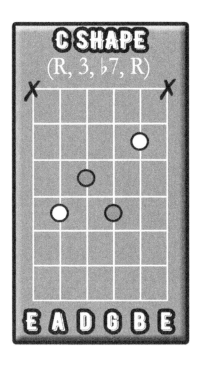

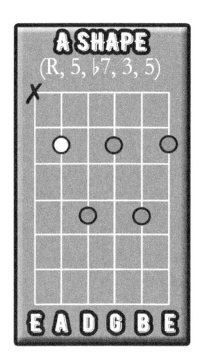

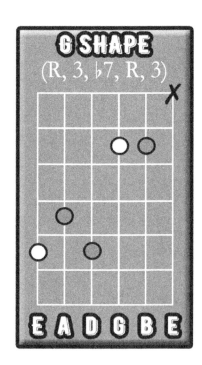

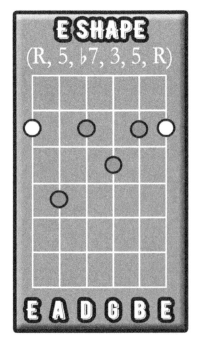

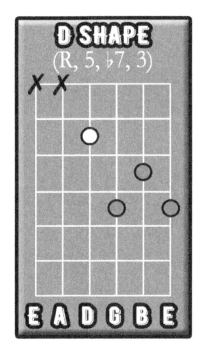

Half-Diminished Chords
Formula (R, ♭3, ♭5, ♭7)

Half-diminished chords, also known as minor seven flat five chords, are formed with the root, minor third, diminished fifth and minor seventh. Using the CAGED system, below are five moveable shapes that allow you to play the same half-diminished seventh chord all over the fretboard. Locrian mode, Locrian natural two and Locrian natural six work well when improvising over this chord.

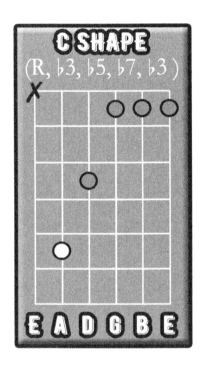

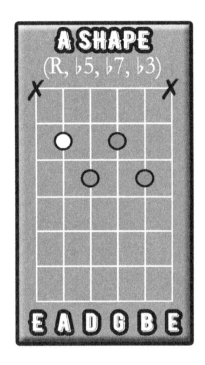

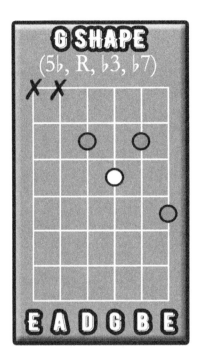

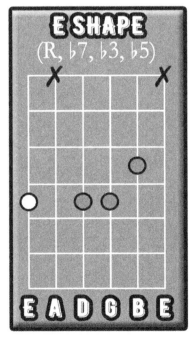

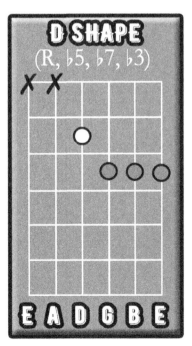

Fully Diminished Seven Chords

Formula (R, b3, b5, bb7)

Diminished seven chords are formed with the root, minor third, diminished fifth and fully diminished/double flat seventh. The fully diminished seventh note is equivalent to a major sixth - to avoid any confusion! Using the CAGED system, below are five moveable shapes that allow you to play the same diminished seventh chord all over the fretboard. Super Locrian (Mode 7) works well when improvising over this chord.

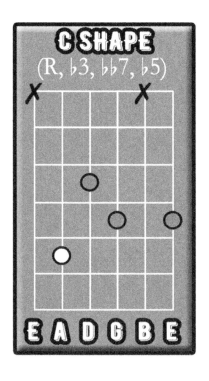

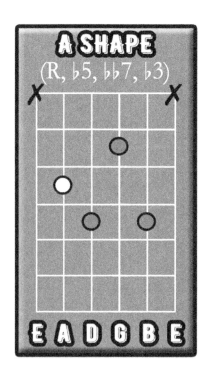

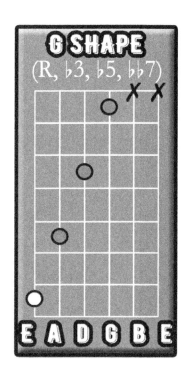

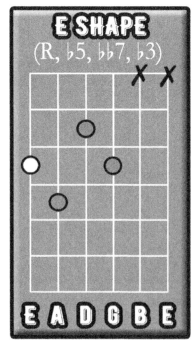

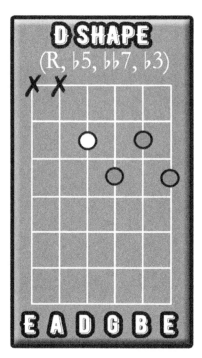

Minor Major Seven Chords
Formula (R, ♭3, 5, 7)

Minor major seven chords are formed with the root, minor third, perfect fifth and major seventh. The minor third gives the chord the minor quality and the natural seven gives it that major sound. Using the CAGED system, below are five moveable shapes that allow you to play the same minor major seventh chord all over the fretboard. Harmonic minor scale works well when improvising over this chord.

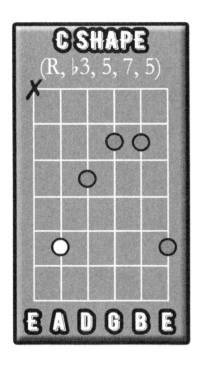

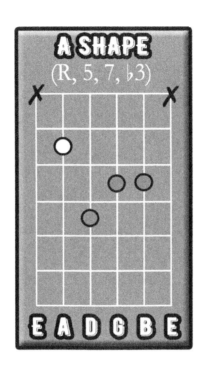

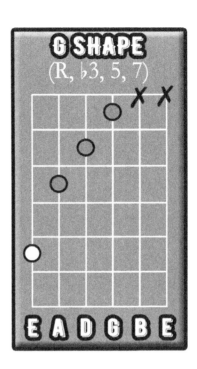

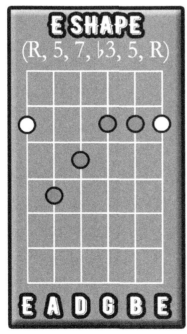

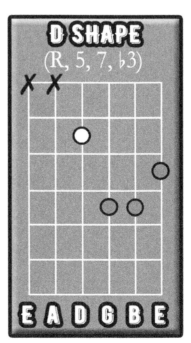

Major Seven Sharp Five Chords
Formula (R, 3, #5, 7)

Major seven sharp five chords are formed with the root, major third, augmented fifth and major seventh. Using the CAGED system, below are five moveable shapes that allow you to play the same major seventh sharp five chord all over the fretboard. Lydian augmented and Ionian sharp five modes work well when improvising over this chord.

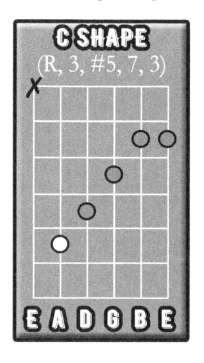

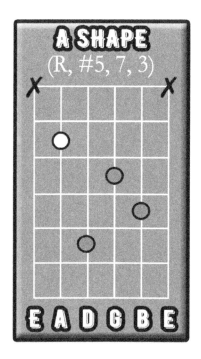

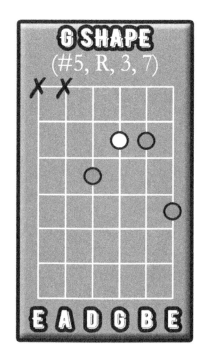

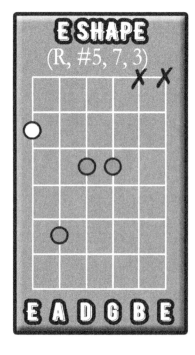

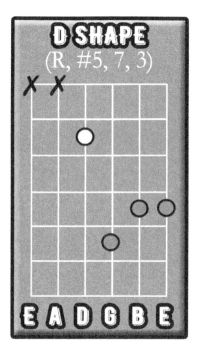

Major Seven Flat Five Chords

Formula (R, 3, ♭5, 7)

Major seven flat five chords are formed with the root, major third, diminished fifth and major seventh. Using the CAGED system, below are five moveable shapes that allow you to play the same major seventh flat five chord all over the fretboard. Lydian mode works well when improvising over this chord.

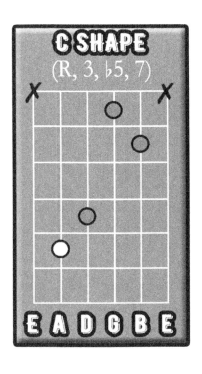

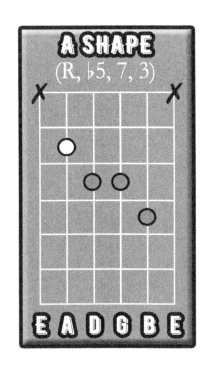

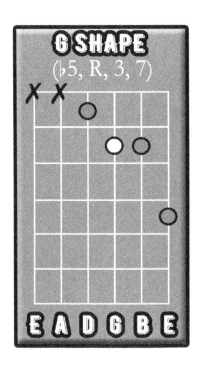

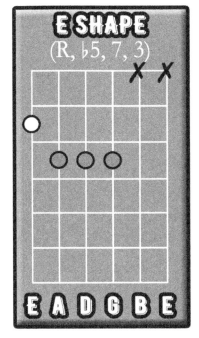

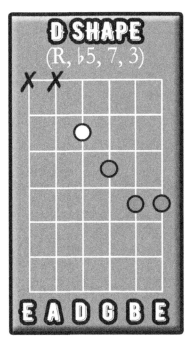

Major Add Nine Chords
Formula (R, 3, 5, 9)

Major add nine chords are formed with the root, major third, perfect fifth, and a ninth. The ninth is actually a major second an octave higher. Using the CAGED system, below are five moveable shapes that allow you to play the same major add nine chord all over the fretboard. The major scale (Ionian mode) and major pentatonic sound great over these chords for improvisation.

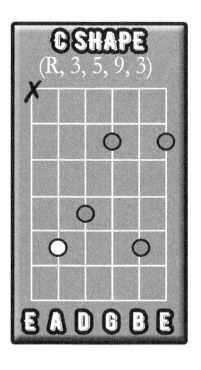

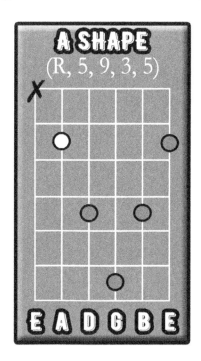

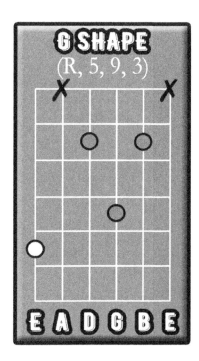

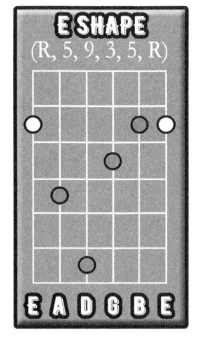

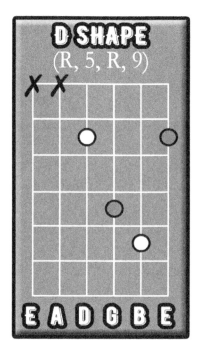

Minor Add Nine Chords

Formula (R, ♭3, 5, 9)

Minor add nine chords are formed with the root, minor third, perfect fifth, and a ninth. The ninth is actually a major second an octave higher. Using the CAGED system, below are five moveable shapes that allow you to play the same minor add nine chord all over the fretboard. The natural minor scale (Aeolian mode), minor pentatonic, blues scale and Dorian mode all sound great for improvisation over these chords.

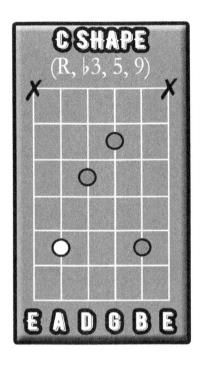

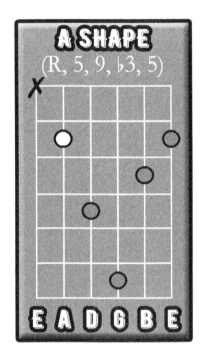

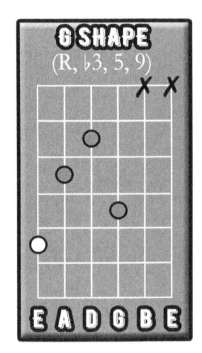

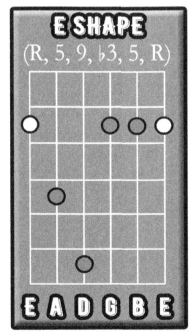

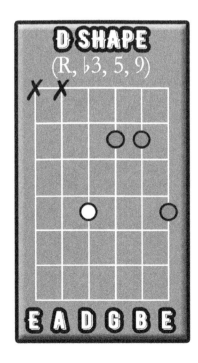

Major Six-Nine Chords
Formula (R, 3, 5, 6, 9)

Major six-nine chords are formed with the root, major third, perfect fifth, major sixth and a ninth. The major ninth is actually a major second an octave up from the root. Using the CAGED system, below are five moveable shapes that allow you to play the same major six-nine chord all over the fretboard. The major scale (Ionian mode) and major pentatonic sound great over these chords for improvisation.

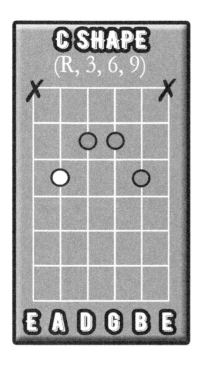

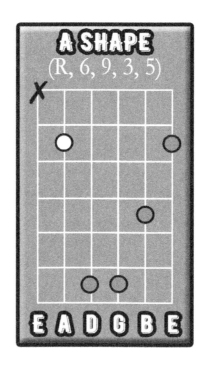

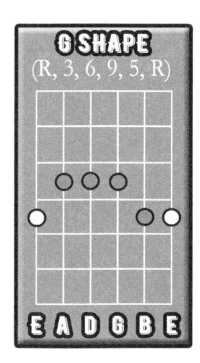

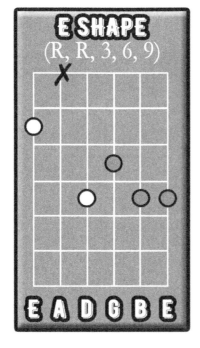

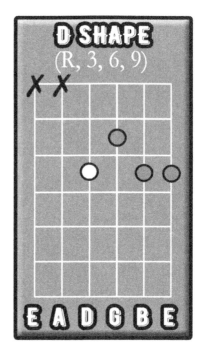

Minor Six-Nine Chords

Formula (R, ♭3, 5, 6, 9)

Minor six-nine chords are formed with the root, minor third, perfect fifth, major sixth and a ninth. The major ninth is actually a major second an octave higher. Using the CAGED system, below are five moveable shapes that allow you to play the same minor six-nine chord all over the fretboard. The natural minor scale (Aeolian mode), minor pentatonic, blues scale and Dorian mode sound great for improvisation over these chords.

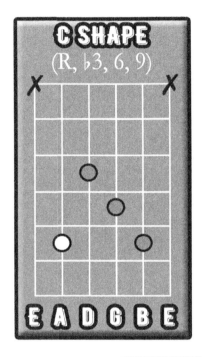

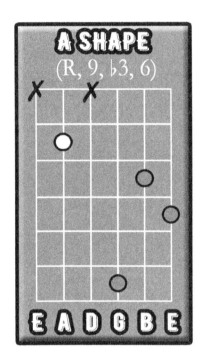

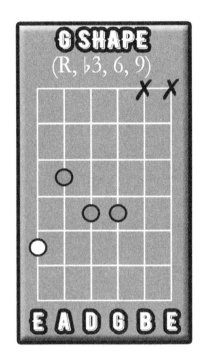

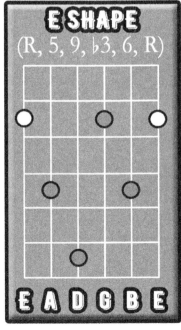

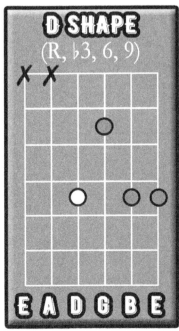

Major Nine Chords
Formula (R, 3, 5, 7, 9)

Major nine chords are formed with the root, major third, perfect fifth, major seventh and a ninth. To make it a true major nine chord and not just a major add nine chord you need to have the seventh in the shape. The major ninth is actually a major second an octave higher, but to make some of these shapes playable and give you the similar sound, I have added the major second in there. Using the CAGED system, below are five moveable shapes that allow you to play the same major ninth chord all over the fretboard. The major scale (Ionian mode) and major pentatonic both sound great over these chords for improvisation.

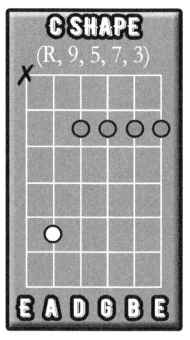

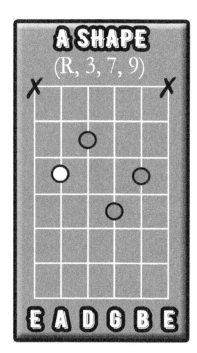

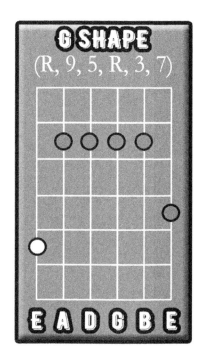

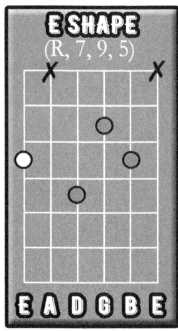

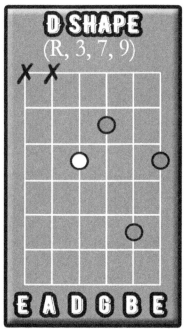

Here are some other really great sounding major nine shapes that I love to use. Personally, major nine is my favourite sounding chord!

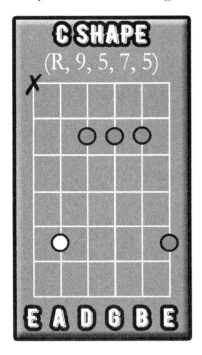

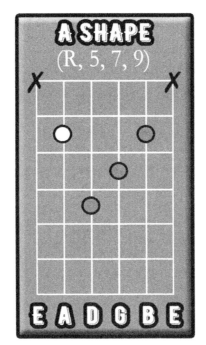

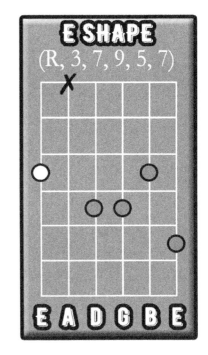

Minor Nine Chords
Formula (R, ♭3, 5, ♭7, 9)

Minor nine chords are formed with the root, minor third, perfect fifth, minor seventh and a ninth. To make it a true minor nine chord, and not just a minor add nine chord, you need to have the seventh in the shape. The major ninth is actually a major second an octave higher. Using the CAGED system, below are five moveable shapes that allow you to play the same minor ninth chord all over the fretboard. The natural minor scale (Aeolian mode), minor pentatonic, blues scale and Dorian mode sound great for improvisation over these chords.

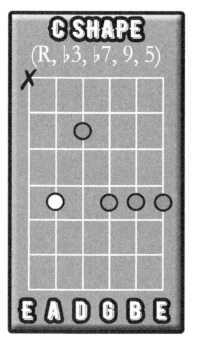

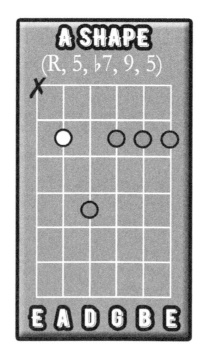

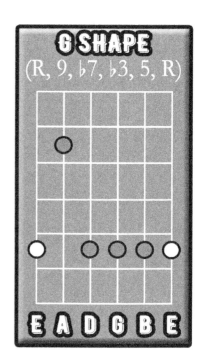

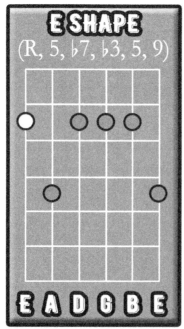

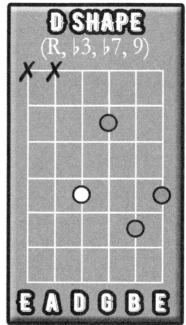

Dominant Nine Chords
Formula (R, 3, 5, ♭7, 9)

Dominant nine chords are formed with the root, major third, perfect fifth, minor seventh and a ninth. The major ninth is actually a major second an octave higher. Using the CAGED system, below are five moveable shapes that allow you to play the same dominant ninth chord all over the fretboard. The major pentatonic, Mixolydian mode, Lydian flat 7 mode, Phrygian Dominant mode and Mixolydian flat six mode all work well for improvising over the top of the chord.

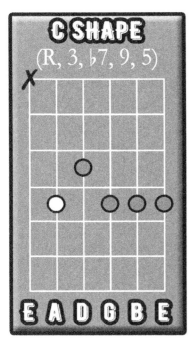

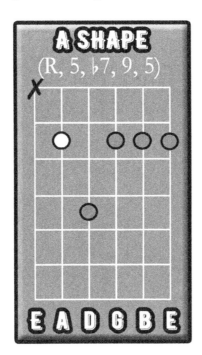

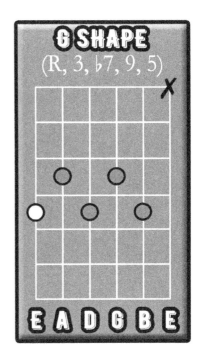

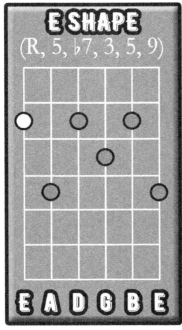

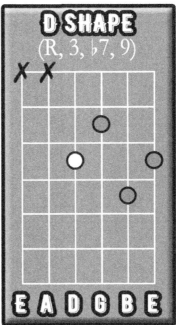

Major Eleven Chords
Formula (R, 3, 5, 7, 9, 11)

Major eleven chords are formed with the root, major third, perfect fifth, major seventh, ninth and eleventh. It is technically impossible to play the six tones of a major eleven chord on guitar, which is why some of the tones are left out from the shapes below. The eleventh is just a fourth an octave higher. Using the CAGED system, below are five moveable shapes that allow you to play the same major eleven chord all over the fretboard. The major scale (Ionian mode) and major pentatonic sounds great over these chords for improvisation.

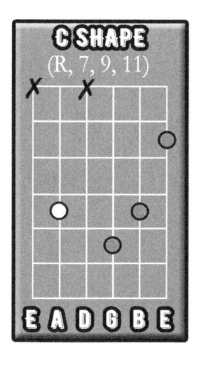

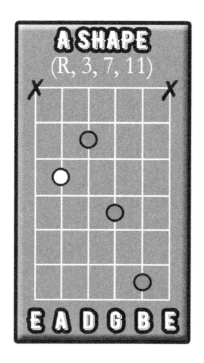

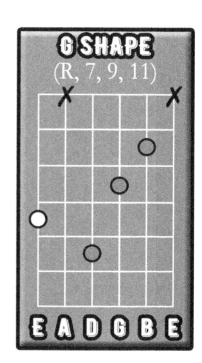

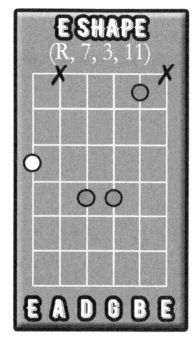

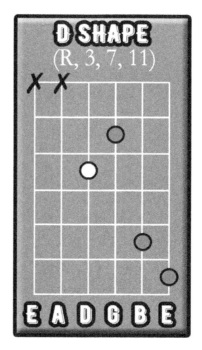

Major Nine Sharp Eleven Chords
Formula (R, 3, 5, 7, 9, #11)

Major nine sharp eleven chords are formed with the root, major third, perfect fifth, major seventh, ninth and sharp eleventh. It is technically impossible to play the six tones of a major nine sharp eleven chord on guitar, which is why some of the less important tones are left out from the shapes below. Using the CAGED system, below are five moveable shapes that allow you to play the same major nine sharp eleven chord all over the fretboard. The major scale (Ionian mode), Lydian mode and major pentatonic all sound great over these chords for improvisation.

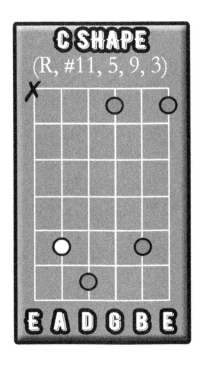

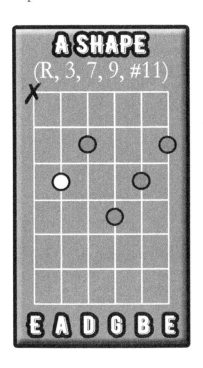

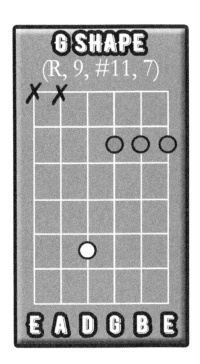

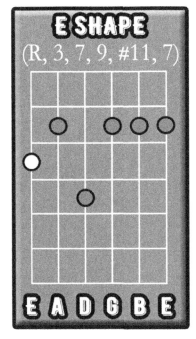

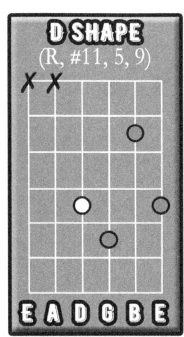

Minor Eleven Chords
Formula (R, ♭3, 5, ♭7, 9, 11)

Minor eleven chords are formed with the root, minor third, perfect fifth, minor seventh, ninth and eleventh. It is technically impossible to play the six tones of a minor eleven chord on guitar, which is why some of the tones are left out from the shapes below. The major eleventh is actually a fourth an octave higher. Using the CAGED system, below are five moveable shapes that allow you to play the same minor eleven chord all over the fretboard. The natural minor scale (Aeolian mode), minor pentatonic, blues scale and Dorian mode sound great for improvisation over these chords.

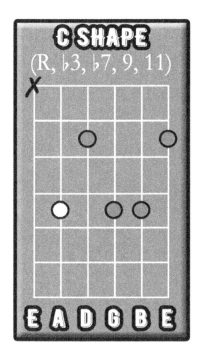

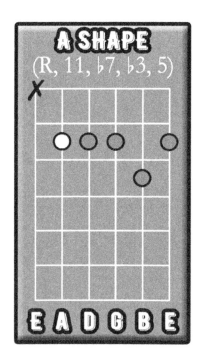

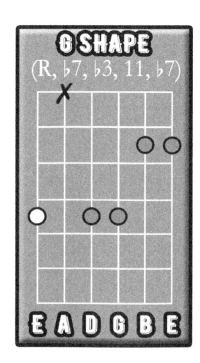

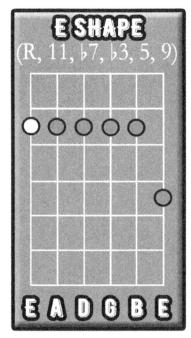

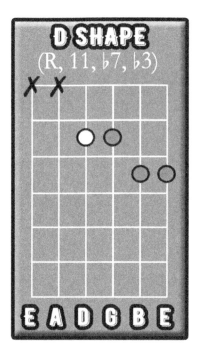

Dominant Eleven Chords
Formula (R, 3, 5, ♭7, 9, 11)

Dominant eleven chords are formed with the root, major third, perfect fifth, minor seventh, ninth and eleventh. It is technically impossible to play the six tones of a dominant eleven chord on guitar, which is why some of the tones are left out from the shapes below. The major eleventh is actually a fourth an octave higher. Using the CAGED system, below are five moveable shapes that allow you to play the same dominant eleven chord all over the fretboard. The major pentatonic, Mixolydian mode, Lydian flat 7 mode, Phrygian Dominant mode and Mixolydian flat six mode all work well for improvising over the top of these chords.

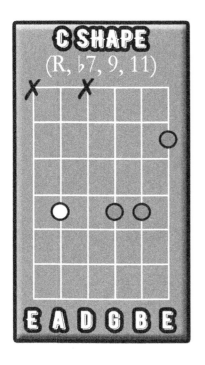

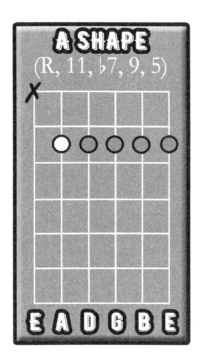

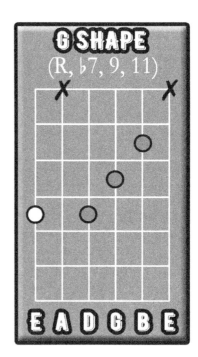

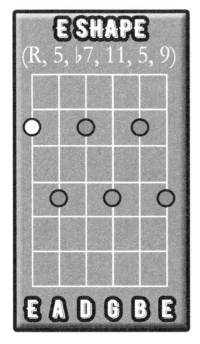

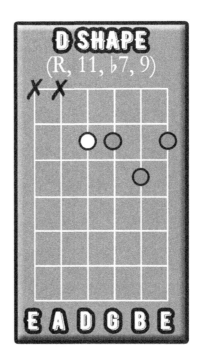

Major Thirteen Chords
Formula (R, 3, 5, 7, 9, 11, 13)

Major thirteen chords are formed with the root, major third, perfect fifth, major seventh, ninth, eleventh and thirteenth. It is technically impossible to play the seven tones of a major thirteen chord on guitar, which is why some of the tones are left out from the shapes below. The thirteenth is a major sixth an octave higher. Using the CAGED system, below are five moveable shapes that allow you to play the same major thirteen chord all over the fretboard. The major scale (Ionian mode) and major pentatonic sound great over these chords for improvisation.

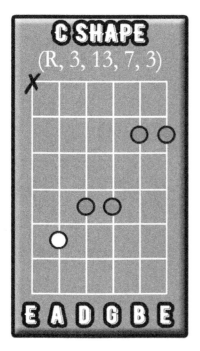

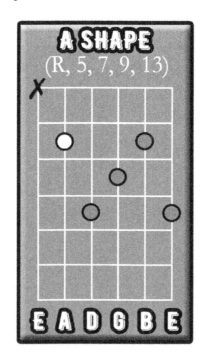

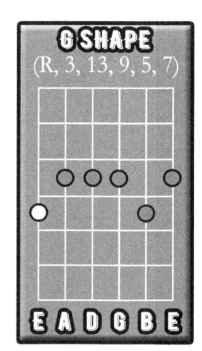

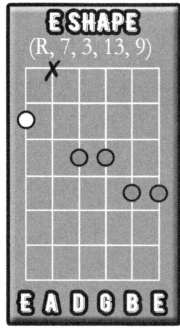

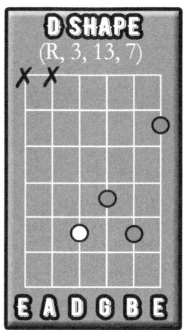

Minor Thirteen Chords
Formula (R, ♭3, 5, ♭7, 9, 11, 13)

Minor thirteen chords are formed with the root, minor third, perfect fifth, minor seventh, ninth, eleventh and thirteenth. It is technically impossible to play the seven tones of a minor thirteen chord on guitar, which is why some of the tones are left out from the shapes below. Using the CAGED system, below are five moveable shapes that allow you to play the same minor thirteen chord all over the fretboard. The natural minor scale (Aeolian mode), minor pentatonic, blues scale and Dorian mode sound great for improvisation over these chords.

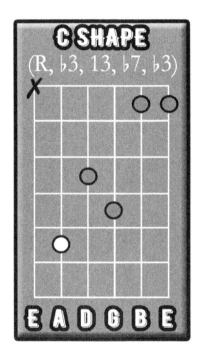

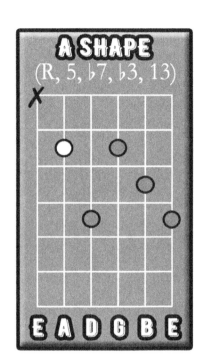

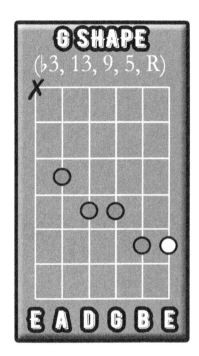

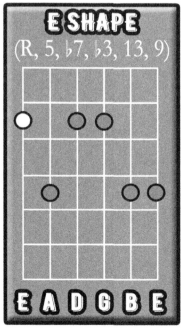

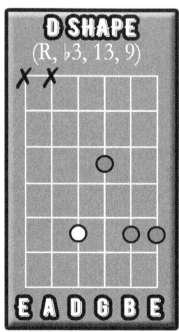

Dominant Thirteen Chords
Formula (R, 3, 5, ♭7, 9, 11, 13)

Dominant thirteen chords are formed with the root, major third, perfect fifth, minor seventh, ninth, eleventh and major thirteenth. It is technically impossible to play the seven tones of a dominant thirteen chord on guitar, which is why some of the tones are left out from the shapes below. Using the CAGED system, below are five moveable shapes that allow you to play the same dominant thirteen chord all over the fretboard. The major pentatonic, Mixolydian mode, Phrygian Dominant mode and Mixolydian flat six mode work well for improvising over the top of these chords.

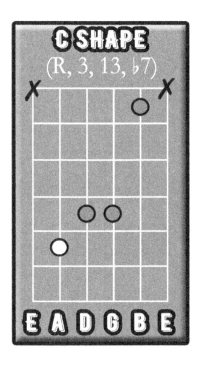

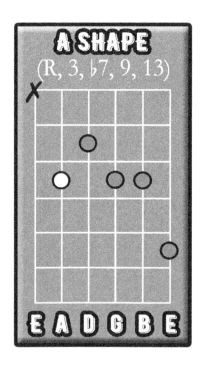

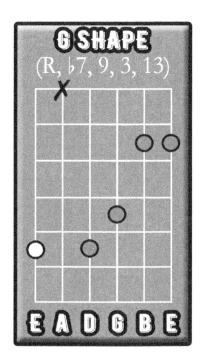

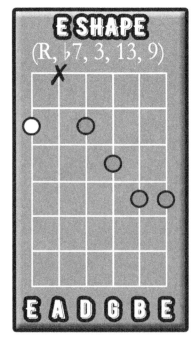

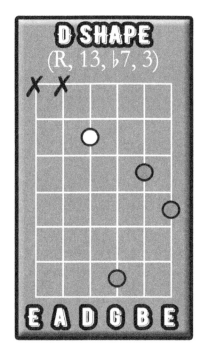

Dominant Thirteen Sus Four Chords

Formula (R, 4, 5, ♭7, 9, 13)

Dominant thirteen sus four chords are formed with the root, perfect fourth, perfect fifth, minor seventh, ninth, and thirteenth. The third has been removed and replaced with a fourth. It is technically impossible to play the seven tones of a dominant thirteen sus four chord on guitar, which is why some of the tones are left out from the shapes below. Using the CAGED system, below are five moveable shapes that allow you to play the same dominant thirteen sus four chord all over the fretboard. The major pentatonic, Mixolydian mode, Phrygian Dominant mode and Mixolydian flat six mode work well for improvising over the top of these chords.

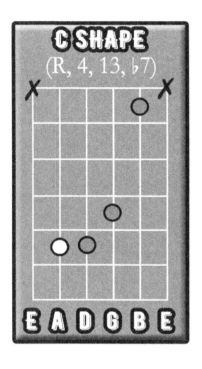

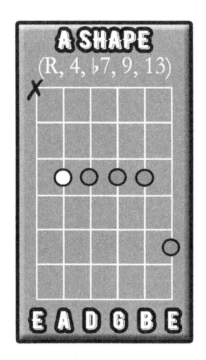

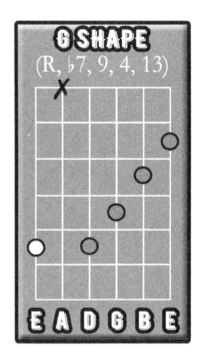

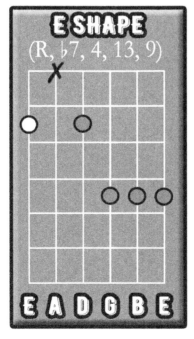

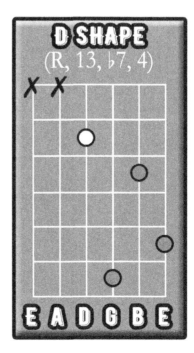

67

Dominant Seven Sharp Five

Formula (R, 3, #5, ♭7)

Dominant seven sharp five chords are formed with the root, major third, augmented fifth and minor seventh. These types of dominant chords where the fifth or ninth (or both) are sharp or flat are known as altered chords. Using the CAGED system, below are five moveable shapes that allow you to play the same dominant seven sharp five chord all over the fretboard. The whole tone scale and the altered scale (7th mode of melodic minor) work well when improvising over these chords.

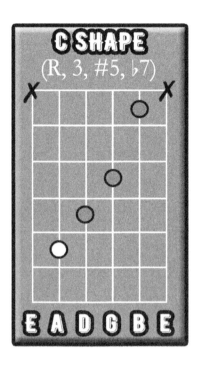

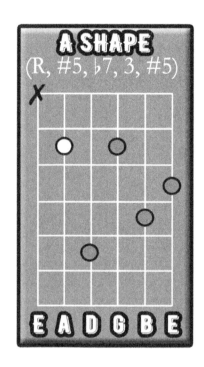

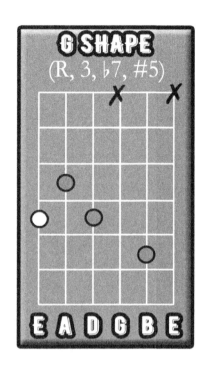

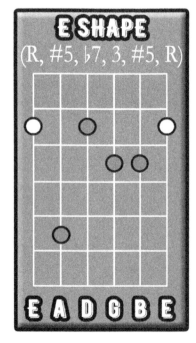

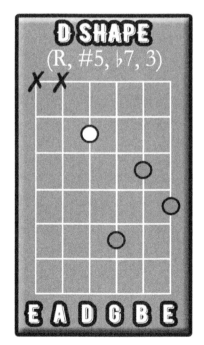

Dominant Seven Sharp Nine

Formula (R, 3, ♭7, #9)

Dominant seven sharp nine chords are formed with the root, major third, minor seventh and sharp ninth. These types of dominant chords where the fifth or ninth (or both) are sharp or flat are known as altered chords. Using the CAGED system, below are five moveable shapes that allow you to play the same dominant seven sharp nine chord all over the fretboard. Minor pentatonic, the minor blues scale, diminished scales, and the altered scale sound great for improvising over these chords.

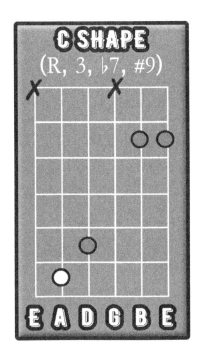

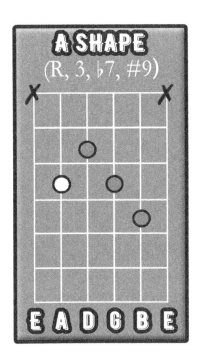

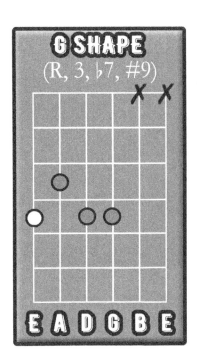

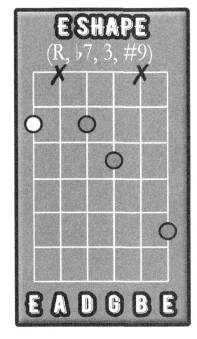

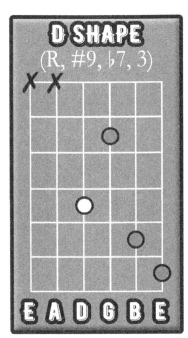

More Altered Chords

Here are some other useful altered shapes that use a mixture of flat and sharp ninths and fifths. Due to the note placements on the guitar it is very hard to create lots of different shapes on the guitar that are playable and sound good.

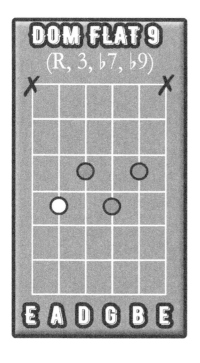

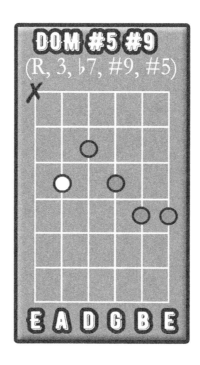

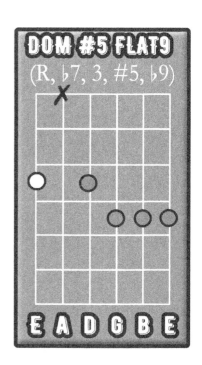

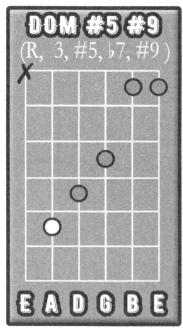

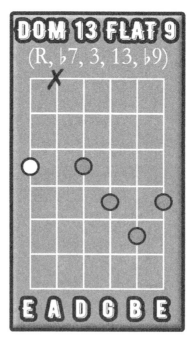

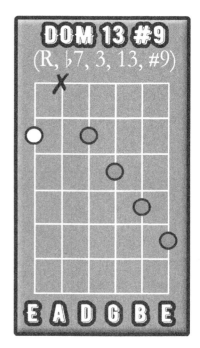

Major Slash Chords

A slash chord has more emphasis on the bass note rather than the root of the chord and they can be a great substitute for basic chords to spice them up. A slash chord can be written with two letters separated by a forward slash such as C/G or D7/C. The first letter is the actual chord name and the second letter, after the slash, is the note to be played in the bass

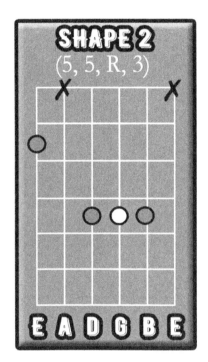

Chord → **D7/C** ← Bass note

Here are some useful major slash chord shapes with some different inversions for you to learn and try out:

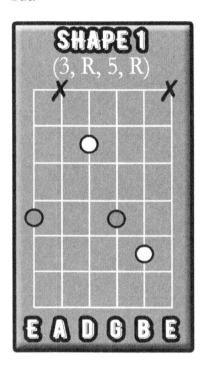

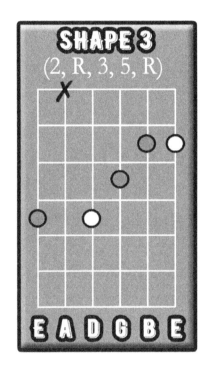

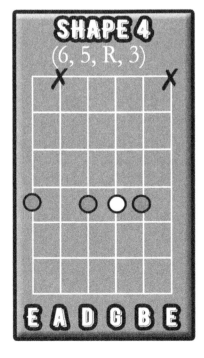

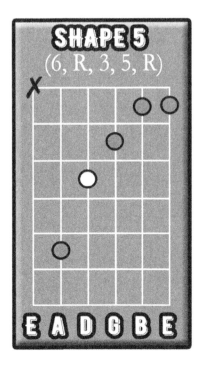

71

Minor Slash Chords

Here are some useful minor slash chord shapes with some different inversions for you to learn and try out:

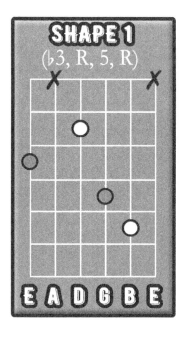
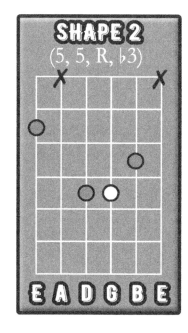
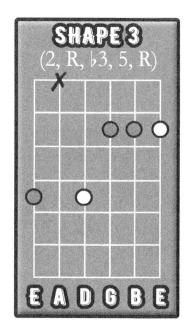

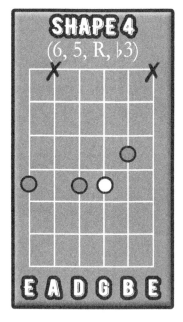
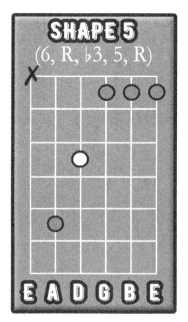

Thumb Chords

The thumb can also be used to fret a note on the low E string. Jimi Hendrix often used this technique for barre chords (E shape from CAGED) which allowed him to have more freedom with his fingers and embellish the chord with some really great lead lines. I have given you examples of the main chord families that you can experiment and have some fun with:

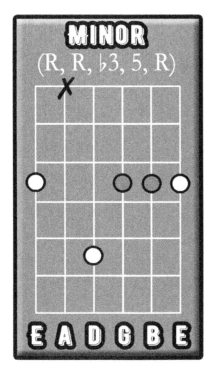

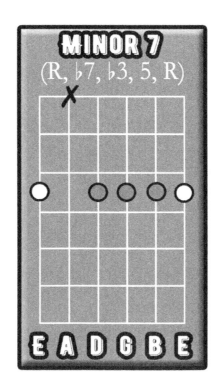

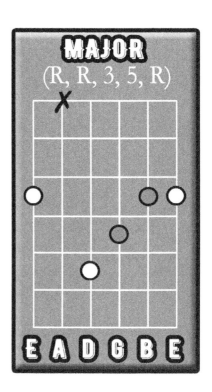

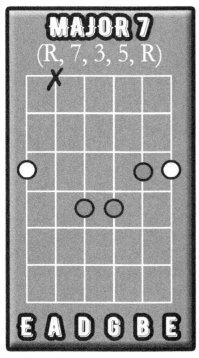

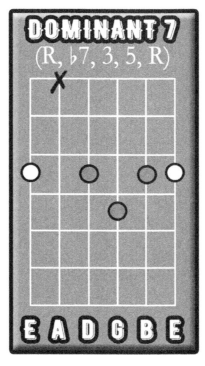

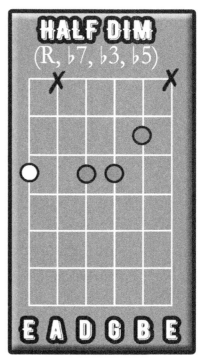

Open Chords

You may have been thinking 'why doesn't this book have any open chords?' – every chord in this book can be moved to an open position. Here are some examples below showing how you can move any shape to the open strings:

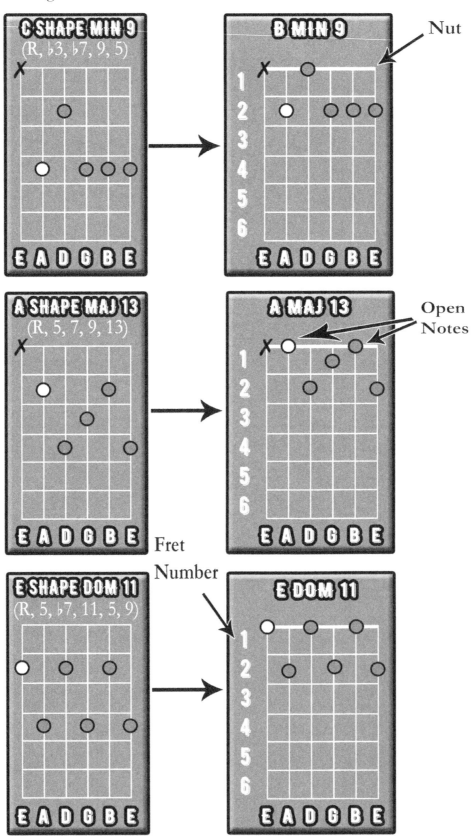

The only issue with moving shapes to be open chords is that you are limiting the keys you use that shape on – unless you use a capo! Below are some examples of moving the same chords to open strings in different keys using a capo:

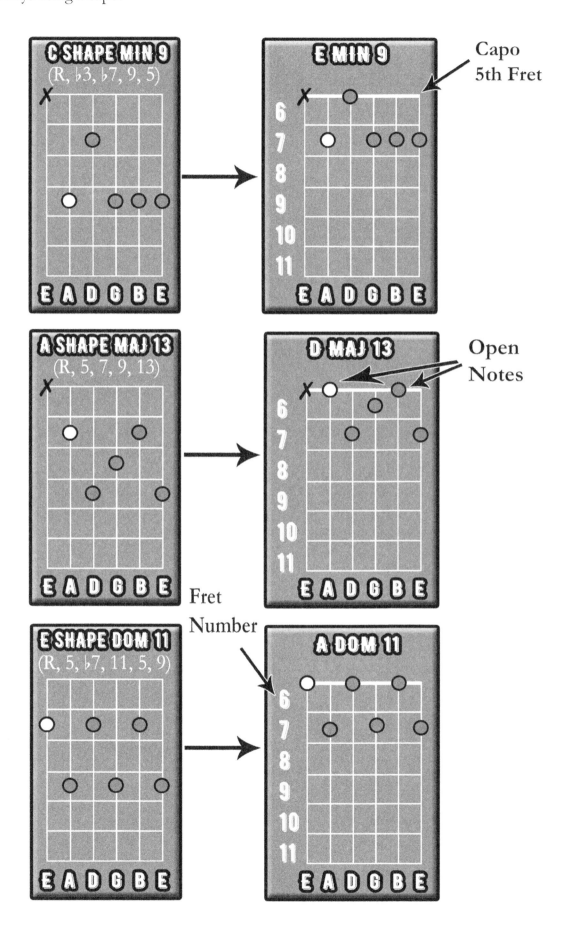

The Most Important Chord Ever!

Formula (R, 5)

You didn't think I would miss out the power chord did you?!?! Although technically it is not a chord as it only has two tonal qualities: the root and fifth, and has no major or minor qualities, but who are we to question the gods of rock 'n' roll?! I have given you the only three shapes you will ever need below…use them wisely! Oh, and you can be even more rock and roll by leaving out the second lower octave!

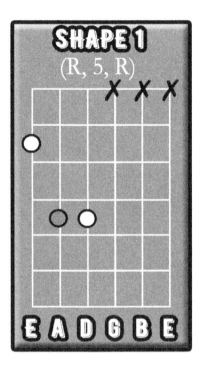

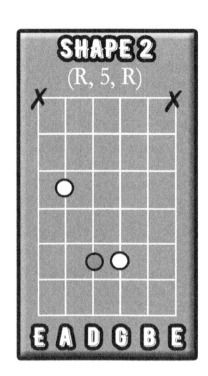

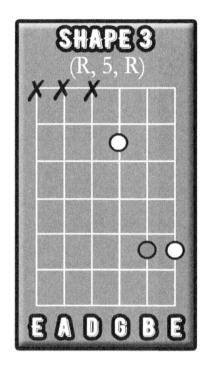

What Is the CAGED System?

The idea of the CAGED system is that you can find any scale, chord, or arpeggio within five or six frets and keep your hand in one position. In this example we will look at the basic major chords, major arpeggios and major scale showing how they connect over the entire fretboard. Hopefully this will help you see how you can apply this to all the chord types in this book. You do not need to understand this to practice the shapes, but it helps!

Let's first take the five basic open major chords **C**, **A**, **G**, **E** and **D**. We want to then link all these basic shapes across the whole fretboard. This then creates every possible shape to play C major. You will need to bar the shapes to recreate the open strings. Once you reach the D shape you will be connected to the C shape again, an octave up, and then the same patterns repeat until you run out of frets.

For every type of chord, arpeggio, and scale, there are five shapes you can connect together.

The next step is to connect the CAGED major scale shaped around these chords.

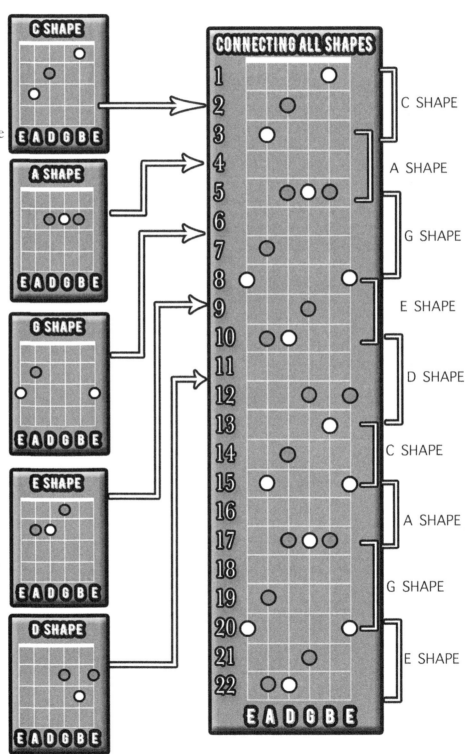

77

Taking our five CAGED major scale shapes, you should now see within them the five CAGED major chord shapes (highlighted below):

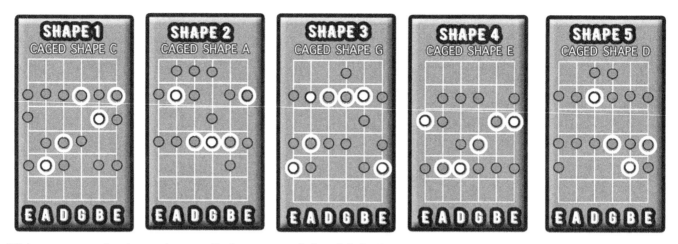

This same method can be applied to any of the CAGED system scales. You just have to learn the CAGED chord shapes that work for that particular scale. For example with the harmonic minor CAGED shapes, after learning all five CAGED shapes for minor-major seventh chords you will see that these chords are embedded in the CAGED shapes. You can even build them yourself using the appropriate chord formulas.

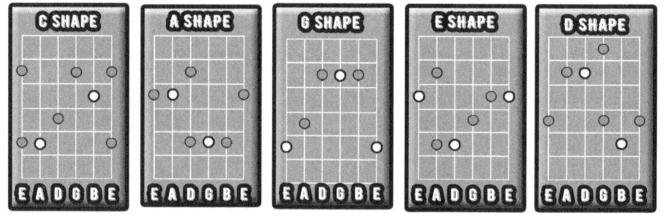

As mentioned earlier you can even play all your arpeggios within the CAGED shapes. Here are all five CAGED major arpeggios:

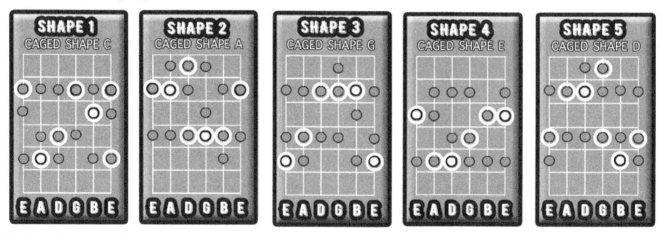

Notice above in the major CAGED scales the embedded chords and arpeggios. This is why the CAGED system is so helpful in connecting the fretboard.

Circle of Fourths & Fifths

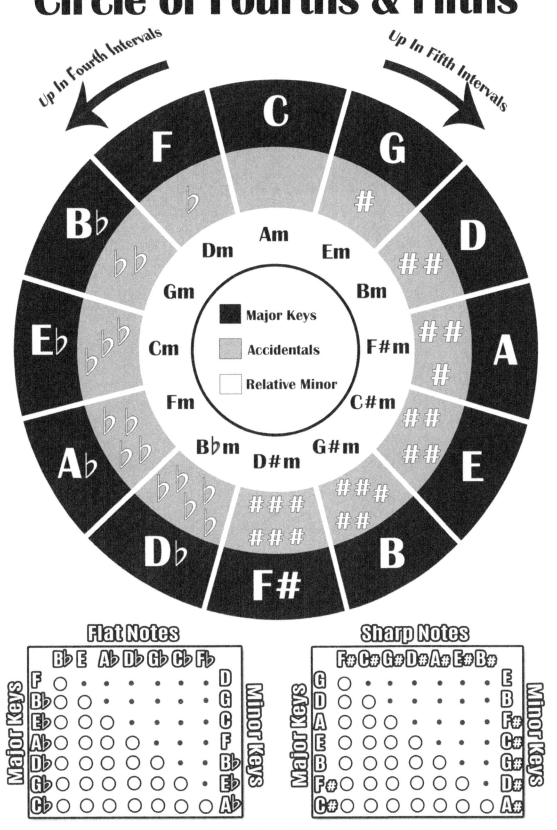

The circle of fifths is a great way to practice the chord shapes in this book in every key. Start with C and make your way round clockwise through the twelve keys.

Writing Chord Progressions

I have put together a fun method to write chord progressions that will help you use the different chords in this book. Don't worry if you do not understand music theory you can use this method without any theory knowledge.

Each of the tables in this chapter has every single possible key on the guitar using the circle of fifths (12 keys). The first table shows basic harmonised major scale chords, then we move onto the more advanced chords harmonising the major scale with sevenths, then ninths, and so on. We also look at minor chords, which is exactly the same as the other charts but you move the VI chord to the I. By harmonising the harmonic and melodic minor, you get a whole new set of chords to explore. This is where things get really interesting!

<u>Using These Tables</u>

First of all, you need to decide a key of the progression you want to use, which is shown in column one under the roman numeral 'I'. Underneath each of the roman numerals is the type of chord it should be such as major, minor, diminished, etc. Most chord progressions sound great starting with the root chord, but don't let that stop you experimenting by starting on any other roman numeral! I quite like starting on the II chord which is minor rather than major. As there are seven notes in the major scale, there are seven corresponding chords.

For example, let's choose a random chord progression I, VI, II and V in the key of C. The chords we would get using the first table 'Harmonised Major Scale' is this;

I – C major
VI – A minor
II – D minor
V – G major

If we did it in the key of F# we would get;

I – F# major
VI – D# minor
II – G# minor
V – C# major

You can now apply any of the chord shapes in this book to this progression and it should sound great. Simply look up the chord family and move the root note to the corresponding note of that chord. Feel free to spice up any of the chords with another related family chord, such as with the C major maybe play a C major 9 instead, or with the A minor try playing A Minor 11. This method can be applied to all the tables in this book!

Harmonised Major Scale
(Major scale or Ionian works over these progressions)

I	II	III	IV	V	VI	VII
Major	Minor	Minor	Major	Major	Minor	Diminished
C	D	E	F	G	A	B
G	A	B	C	D	E	F#
D	E	F#	G	A	B	C#
A	B	C#	D	E	F#	G#
E	F#	G#	A	B	C#	D#
B	C#	D#	E	F#	G#	A#
F#	G#	A#	B	C#	D#	E#
Db	Eb	F	Gb	Ab	Bb	C
Ab	Bb	C	Db	Eb	F	G
Eb	F	G	Ab	Bb	C	D
Bb	C	D	Eb	F	G	A
F	G	A	Bb	C	D	E

Harmonised Major Scale 7th Degree
(Major scale or Ionian works over these progressions)

I	II	III	IV	V	VI	VII
Maj7	Min7	Min7	Maj7	Dom7	Min7	Half-Diminished
C	D	E	F	G	A	B
G	A	B	C	D	E	F#
D	E	F#	G	A	B	C#
A	B	C#	D	E	F#	G#
E	F#	G#	A	B	C#	D#
B	C#	D#	E	F#	G#	A#
F#	G#	A#	B	C#	D#	E#
Db	Eb	F	Gb	Ab	Bb	C
Ab	Bb	C	Db	Eb	F	G
Eb	F	G	Ab	Bb	C	D
Bb	C	D	Eb	F	G	A
F	G	A	Bb	C	D	E

Harmonised Major Scale 9th Degree
(Major scale or Ionian works over these progressions)

I Maj9	II Min9	III Min7♭9	IV Maj9	V Dom9	VI Min9	VII Half-Dimi ♭9
C	D	E	F	G	A	B
G	A	B	C	D	E	F#
D	E	F#	G	A	B	C#
A	B	C#	D	E	F#	G#
E	F#	G#	A	B	C#	D#
B	C#	D#	E	F#	G#	A#
F#	G#	A#	B	C#	D#	E#
D♭	E♭	F	G♭	A♭	B♭	C
A♭	B♭	C	D♭	E♭	F	G
E♭	F	G	A♭	B♭	C	D
B♭	C	D	E♭	F	G	A
F	G	A	B♭	C	D	E

Harmonised Minor Scale 7th Degree
(Natural minor scale known as Aeolian mode works over these progressions)

I Min7	II Half-Diminished	III Maj7	IV Min7	V Min7	VI Maj7	VII Dom7
A	B	C	D	E	F	G
E	F#	G	A	B	C	D
B	C#	D	E	F#	G	A
F#	G#	A	B	C#	D	E
C#	D#	E	F#	G#	A	B
G#	A#	B	C#	D#	E	F#
D#	E#	F#	G#	A#	B	C#
B♭	C	D♭	E♭	F	G♭	A♭
F	G	A♭	B♭	C	D♭	E♭
C	D	E♭	F	G	A♭	B♭
G	A	B♭	C	D	E♭	F
D	E	F	G	A	B♭	C

Harmonised Harmonic Minor Scale
(Harmonic minor scale works over these progressions)

I Min(Maj)7	II Half-Diminished	III Maj7#5	IV Min7	V Dom7	VI Maj7	VII Fully-Diminished
C	D	Eb	F	G	Ab	B
G	A	Bb	C	D	Eb	F#
D	E	F	G	A	Bb	C#
A	B	C	D	E	F	G#
E	F#	G	A	B	C	D#
B	C#	D	E	F#	G	A#
F#	G#	A	B	C#	D	E#
C#	D#	E	F#	G#	A	C
G#	A#	B	C#	D#	E	G
D#	F	F#	G#	A#	B	D
A#	C	C#	D#	F	F#	A
F	G	Ab	Bb	C	Db	E

Harmonised Melodic Minor Scale
(Melodic minor scale works over these progressions)

I Min(Maj)7	II Min7	III Maj7#5	IV Dom7	V Dom7	VI Half-Diminished	VII Half-Diminished
C	D	Eb	F	G	A	B
G	A	Bb	C	D	E	F#
D	E	F	G	A	B	C#
A	B	C	D	E	F#	G#
E	F#	G	A	B	C#	D#
B	C#	D	E	F#	G#	A#
F#	G#	A	B	C#	D#	E#
C#	D#	E	F#	G#	A#	C
G#	A#	B	C#	D#	F	G
D#	F	F#	G#	A#	C	D
A#	C	C#	D#	F	G	A
F	G	Ab	Bb	C	D	E

10 Common Chord Progressions

Using the harmonised major seventh scale chords, here are some of the most memorable and catchy chord progressions that are used in popular music today to try out in your song writing. I will use the key of C for examples of chords to use, but of course you can transpose these to any key using the charts in the previous section of this book. Feel free to swap out some of the chords for extended chords such as minor nines, major elevens, dominant thirteens, etc.

1.

I	V	VI	IV
Cmaj7	Gdom7	Amin7	Fmaj7

2.

I	IV	VI	V
Cmaj7	Fmaj7	Amin7	Gdom7

3.

I	V	VI
Cmaj7	Gdom7	Amin7

4.

I	III	II	VII
Cmaj7	Emin7	Dmin7	Bmin7b5

5.

VI	IV	V	I
Amin7	Fmaj7	Gdom7	Cmaj7

6.

VI	IV	I	V
Amin7	Fmaj7	Cmaj7	Gdom7

7.

II	VI	IV	I
Dmin7	Amin7	Fmaj7	Cmaj7

8.

VI	II	IV	V
Amin7	Dmin7	Fmaj7	Gdom7

9.

VI	I	IV	V
Amin7	Cmaj7	Fmaj7	Gdom7

10.

IV	V	VI
Fmaj7	Gdom7	Amin7

You will find these chord progressions in many pop songs that use even just the basic harmonised major scale with basic major or minor chords. Experiment and have fun writing your own progressions and if you are feeling adventurous you can try changing keys by using connecting chords, for example if you are in the key of C and you play the II chord, which is E minor, in the key of G the E minor chord is the VI chord. You can then use chords after this in that key, creating a bridge!

Creating Your Own Shapes

Over the next few pages are some empty charts and blank tablature where you can create your own shapes or make some alterations to the shapes in this book.

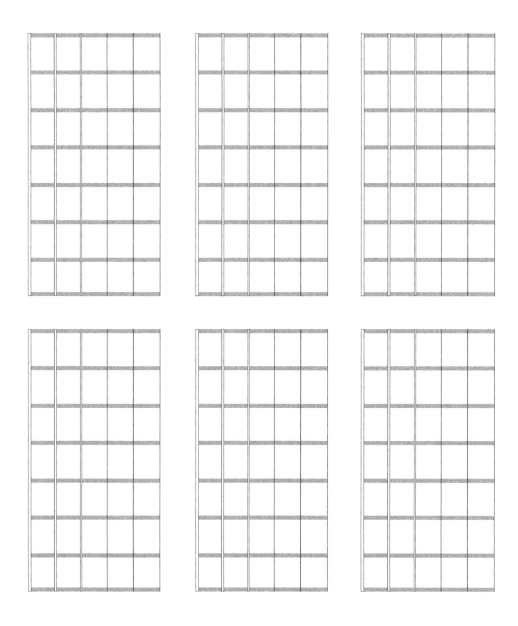

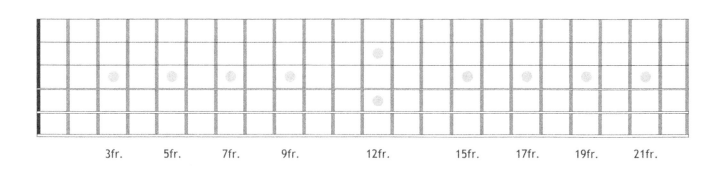

3fr.   5fr.   7fr.   9fr.   12fr.   15fr.   17fr.   19fr.   21fr.

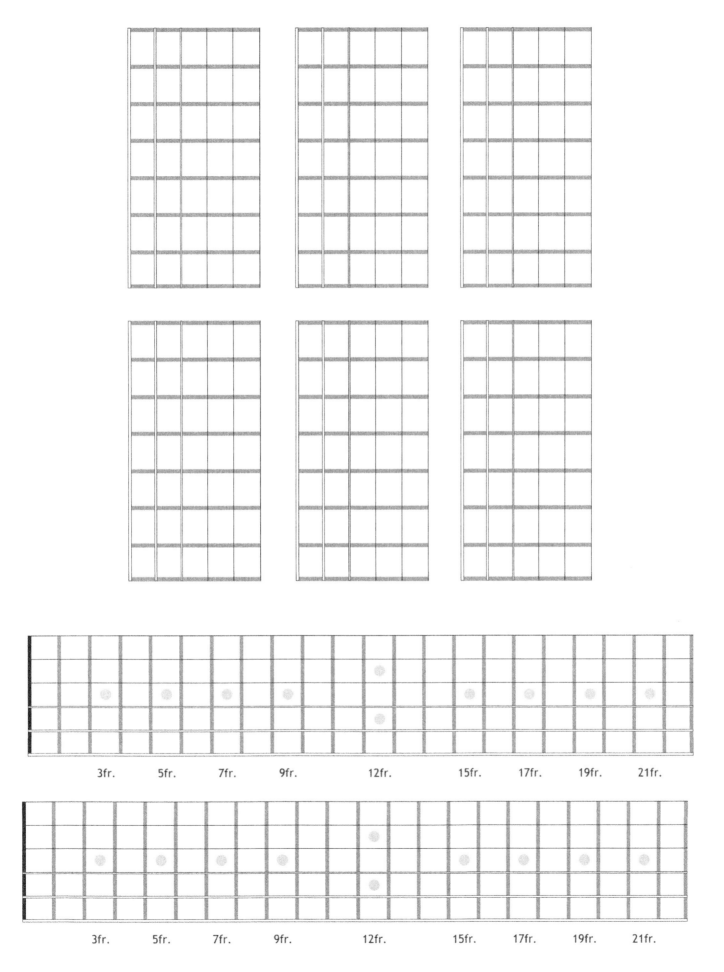

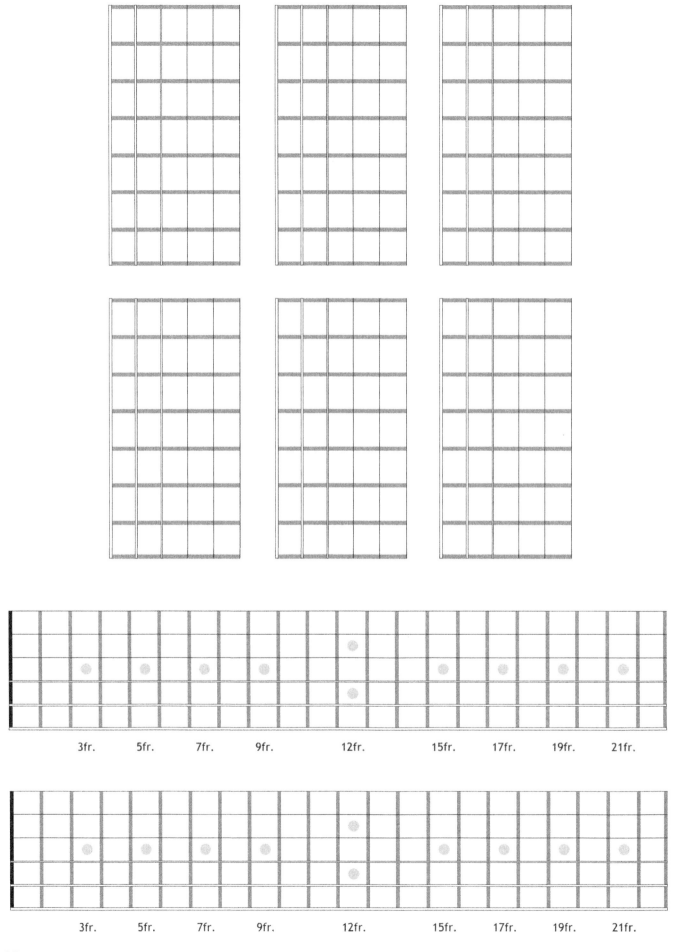

3fr.   5fr.   7fr.   9fr.   12fr.   15fr.   17fr.   19fr.   21fr.

3fr.   5fr.   7fr.   9fr.   12fr.   15fr.   17fr.   19fr.   21fr.

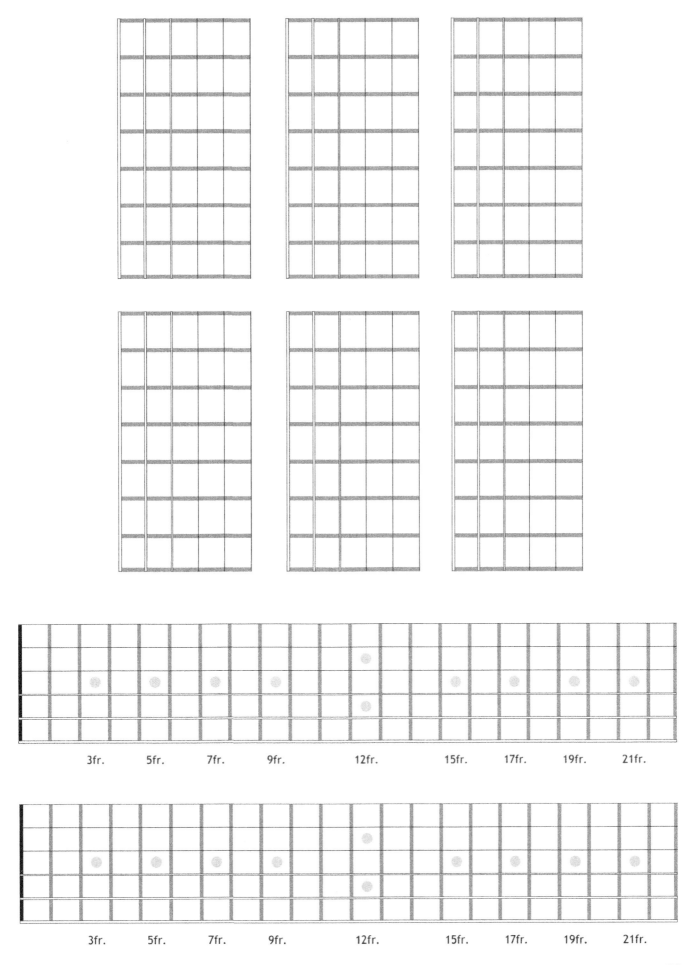

Practice Diary

It is very important to maintain a good practice routine by keeping track of your goals and progress. By doing this you can feel a real sense of achievement and look back on how far you have progressed. I recommend keeping track of what shapes you have learned and what you have discovered.

Week: _____

Goals This Week:

_____

_____

_____

_____

Achievements This Week:

_____

_____

_____

_____

Things To Work On Next Week:

_____

_____

_____

_____

Notes:

_____

_____

_____

_____

Week: _____

Goals This Week:

_____

_____

_____

_____

Achievements This Week:

_____

_____

_____

_____

Things To Work On Next Week:

_____

_____

_____

_____

Notes:

_____

_____

_____

_____

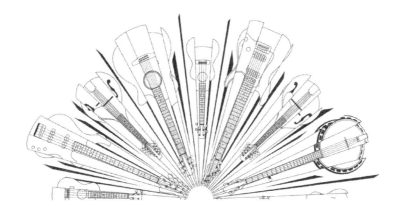

Week: _____

Goals This Week:

_____
_____
_____
_____

Achievements This Week:

_____
_____
_____
_____

Things To Work On Next Week:

_____
_____
_____
_____

Notes:

_____
_____
_____
_____

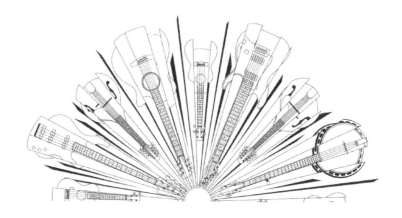

Week: _____

Goals This Week:

_____

_____

_____

_____

Achievements This Week:

_____

_____

_____

_____

Things To Work On Next Week:

_____

_____

_____

_____

Notes:

_____

_____

_____

_____

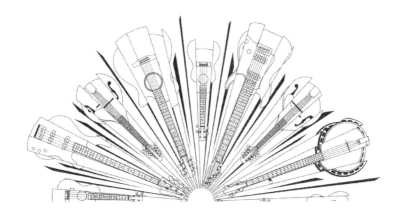

Week: _____

Goals This Week:

_____

_____

_____

_____

Achievements This Week:

_____

_____

_____

_____

Things To Work On Next Week:

_____

_____

_____

_____

Notes:

_____

_____

_____

_____

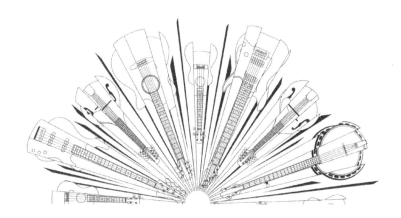

Week: _____

Goals This Week:

_____

_____

_____

_____

Achievements This Week:

_____

_____

_____

_____

Things To Work On Next Week:

_____

_____

_____

_____

Notes:

_____

_____

_____

_____

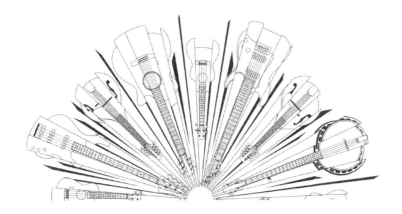

Week: _____

Goals This Week:

_____

_____

_____

_____

Achievements This Week:

_____

_____

_____

_____

Things To Work On Next Week:

_____

_____

_____

_____

Notes:

_____

_____

_____

_____

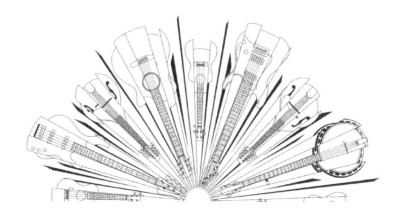

Week: _____

Goals This Week:

_____

_____

_____

_____

Achievements This Week:

_____

_____

_____

_____

Things To Work On Next Week:

_____

_____

_____

_____

Notes:

_____

_____

_____

_____

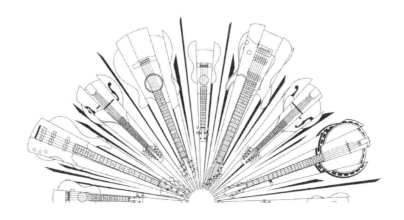

Week: _____

Goals This Week:

_____

_____

_____

_____

Achievements This Week:

_____

_____

_____

_____

Things To Work On Next Week:

_____

_____

_____

_____

Notes:

_____

_____

_____

_____

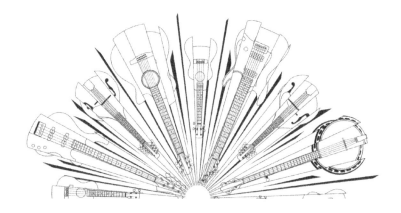

Week: _____

Goals This Week:

_____

_____

_____

_____

Achievements This Week:

_____

_____

_____

_____

Things To Work On Next Week:

_____

_____

_____

_____

Notes:

_____

_____

_____

_____

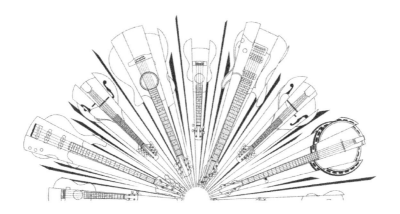

Week: _____

Goals This Week:

_____

_____

_____

_____

Achievements This Week:

_____

_____

_____

_____

Things To Work On Next Week:

_____

_____

_____

_____

Notes:

_____

_____

_____

_____

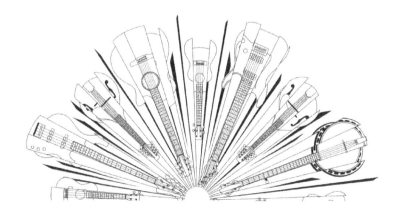

Week: _____

Goals This Week:

_____

_____

_____

_____

Achievements This Week:

_____

_____

_____

_____

Things To Work On Next Week:

_____

_____

_____

_____

Notes:

_____

_____

_____

_____

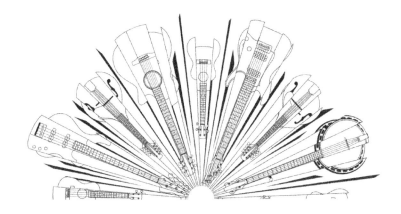

Week: _____

Goals This Week:

_____

_____

_____

_____

Achievements This Week:

_____

_____

_____

_____

Things To Work On Next Week:

_____

_____

_____

_____

Notes:

_____

_____

_____

_____

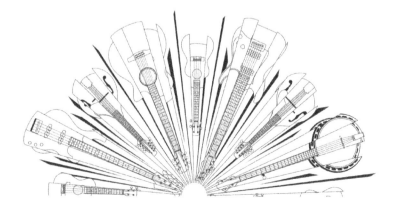

Week: _____

Goals This Week:

_____
_____
_____
_____

Achievements This Week:

_____
_____
_____
_____

Things To Work On Next Week:

_____
_____
_____
_____

Notes:

_____
_____
_____
_____

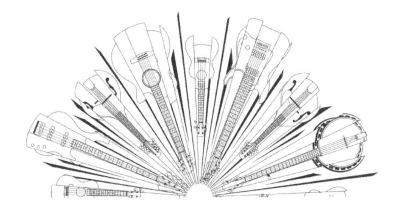

Week: _____

Goals This Week:

_____

_____

_____

_____

Achievements This Week:

_____

_____

_____

_____

Things To Work On Next Week:

_____

_____

_____

_____

Notes:

_____

_____

_____

_____

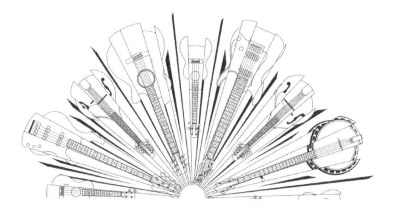

Week: _____

Goals This Week:

_____

_____

_____

_____

Achievements This Week:

_____

_____

_____

_____

Things To Work On Next Week:

_____

_____

_____

_____

Notes:

_____

_____

_____

_____

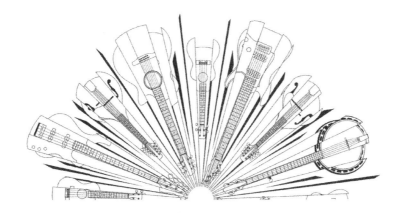

Week: _____

Goals This Week:

_____

_____

_____

_____

Achievements This Week:

_____

_____

_____

_____

Things To Work On Next Week:

_____

_____

_____

_____

Notes:

_____

_____

_____

_____

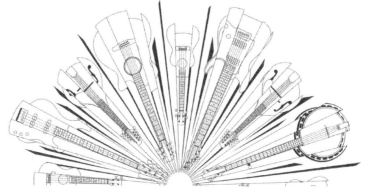

Week: _____

Goals This Week:

_____
_____
_____
_____

Achievements This Week:

_____
_____
_____
_____

Things To Work On Next Week:

_____
_____
_____
_____

Notes:

_____
_____
_____
_____

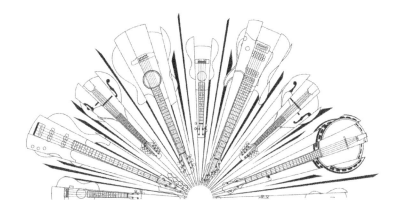

Week: _____

Goals This Week:

_____

_____

_____

_____

Achievements This Week:

_____

_____

_____

_____

Things To Work On Next Week:

_____

_____

_____

_____

Notes:

_____

_____

_____

_____

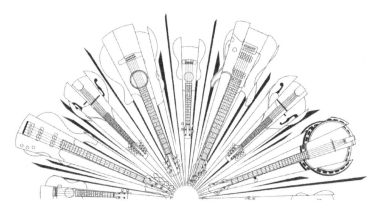

Week: _____

Goals This Week:

_____

_____

_____

_____

Achievements This Week:

_____

_____

_____

_____

Things To Work On Next Week:

_____

_____

_____

_____

Notes:

_____

_____

_____

_____

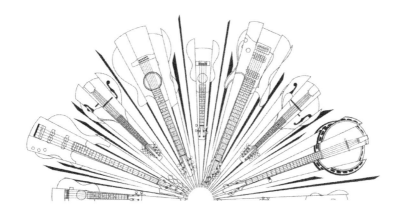

Week: _____

Goals This Week:

_____

_____

_____

_____

Achievements This Week:

_____

_____

_____

_____

Things To Work On Next Week:

_____

_____

_____

_____

Notes:

_____

_____

_____

_____

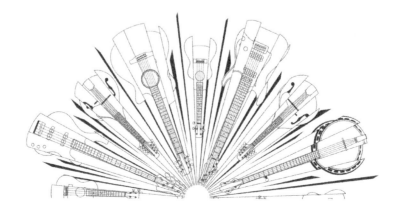

Week: _____

Goals This Week:

_____

_____

_____

_____

Achievements This Week:

_____

_____

_____

_____

Things To Work On Next Week:

_____

_____

_____

_____

Notes:

_____

_____

_____

_____

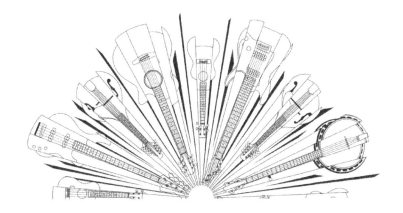

The Ultimate Guitar Series

Don't forget to check out the other books in 'The Ultimate Guitar Series'

-The Ultimate Guitar Scales Book-

Going from the simplest scales, such as the Minor Pentatonic scale, through to the more complex, such as Harmonic Minor and Melodic Minor scales, this book uses 3-note per string and CAGED shapes to connect the different shapes across the whole fretboard. This book can be used simply as a reference point for shapes to play for certain scales/modes, or to further develop your knowledge and practice routines to become the ultimate guitar player!

-The Ultimate Guitar Arpeggio Book-

With this book we are looking at arpeggio shapes starting from the most basic triad arpeggios to the more advanced extended arpeggios such as ninths, elevenths and thirteenths. So many arpeggio books I have read in the past have hundreds of unnecessary shapes that are just repeated in every key. This can be confusing and make players think they have a massive volume of arpeggio shapes to learn, which they don't.

-The Ultimate Guitar Sweep Picking Book-

Sweep picking can be one of the most daunting techniques to learn and play and speaking from experience I understand the frustrations of not knowing what shapes are best to learn and play! This book gives you all the tools you need to understand how to build your own sweep picking licks and become a master of the sweeps in no time! Jumping straight to the juicy bits focusing on arpeggio shapes specifically for sweep picking that loop in bars of 4/4 and are movable to any key! Whether new to sweep picking or a more advanced player this book is the ultimate sweep picking reference book for inspiration.

All my books are dedicated to my wife Lisa and my daughter Abigail

GUITAR TABS GLOSSARY

TABLATURE (TABS) EXPLAINED

Tablature illustrates the six strings on the guitar. Notes and chords are represented by the placement of fret numbers on each given string(s).

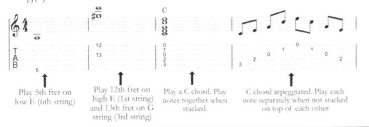

Play 5th fret on low E (6th string)

Play 12th fret on high E (1st string) and 13th fret on G string (3rd string)

Play a C chord. Play notes together when stacked.

C chord arpeggiated. Play each note separately when not stacked on top of each other

---

BENDING NOTES

SLIGHT BEND

Play the note and bend it slightly to the equivalent of half a fret.

HALF STEP

Play the note and bend bend string one half step. Equivalent of one fret.

WHOLE STEP

Play the note and bend bend string one whole step. Equivalent of two frets.

WHOLE STEP & A HALF

Play the note and bend bend string whole step and a half. Equivalent of three frets.

TWO STEPS

Play the note and bend bend string two whole steps. Equivalent of four frets.

BEND AND RELEASE

Play the note and bend it then release back down to the original note.

PREBEND

Bend the string to specific note and then pick note.

PREBEND AND RELEASE

Bend the string, play it, then release to the original note.

PREBEND AND BEND

Bend the string, play it, then bend to next note.

A half step is the smallest interval in western music which is equal to one fret. A whole step equals two frets.

BENDS INVOLVING MORE THAN ONE STRING

Play the note and bend the string while playing additional note(s) on other strings

UNISON BENDS

Play both notes and immediately bend the lower note to the same pitch as the higher note.

DOUBLE NOTE BENDS

Play both notes and immediately bend both strings simultaneously.

BENDS WITH STATIONARY NOTES

Play notes and bend lower pitch, then hold until released back to original note.

HARMONICS

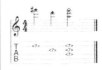

NATURAL HARMONICS

A finger of the fretting hand lightly touches the note or notes indicated in the tab and then picked. Place finger just over the fret to get best sound.

ARTIFICIAL HARMONICS

The first tab number is fretted then the pick hand produces the harmonic by using a finger to touch lightly the same string in the second tab in brackets and then picked with another finger.

PINCHED HARMONICS

The first note is fretted then the pick hand produces the harmonics by squeezing the pick firmly while using the tip of the index finger in the pick attack. The note in the brackets is the pitch that should be created.

TAPPED HARMONICS

The first tab number is fretted then the pick hand produces the harmonic by using a finger to tap on the note in the brackets.

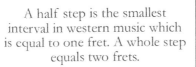

ARTICULATIONS

HAMMER ON

Play lower note, then "hammer on" to higher note with another finger. Only the first note is picked.

PULL OFF

Play higher note, then "pull off" to lower note with another finger. Only the first note is picked.

HAMMER ON FROM NOWHERE

Hammer on first note (T) with fretting hand. No picking used with hammer ons from nowhere.

FINGER TAPPING

Not to be confused with the hammer on from nowhere this uses a finger from the picking hand to tap the note indicated with the "T" and then pull off to the next notes held by the fretting hand.

SLAP & POP

Use your thumb of your picking hand to hit down or 'slap' the note in the tabs (s). Use your index finger of your picking hand to pluck or 'pop' the note in the tab (p).

LEFT HAND FINGERING

This indicates which fingers to use with your fretting hand.
1 = Index
2 = Middle
3 = Ring Finger
4 = Pinky
T = Thumb
0 = No fingers!

LEGATO SLIDE

Play note and slide to the next note. Only the first note is picked.

WAH WAH PEDAL

'O' means to close your wah (foot up) and '+' means to open your wah (foot down)

TREMOLO PICKING

The note or notes are picked as fast as possible using alternate picking.

VIBRATO

The pitch of a note is alliterated slightly by a rapid shaking of the fretting hand finger. Can be vertical, horizontal or circular vibrato.

DOWN & UP STROKES

Notes or chords are to be played with either a:
⊓ = Downstroke
V = Upstroke

RIGHT HAND FINGERING

This indicates which fingers to use with your picking hand.
p = Thumb
i = Index
m = Middle
a = Ring Finger
c = Pinky

MUTED STRINGS

A percussive sound is made by laying the fretting hand across all six strings while your picking hand strikes the specific strings in tabs.

PALM MUTE

The note or notes are muted by the palm of the picking hand by lightly touching the strings near the bridge of the guitar,

TRILL

Hammer on and pull off consecutively and as fast as possible between the original note and the grace note.

ACCENT

Notes or chords are to be played with added emphasis.

STACCATO

Notes or chords are to be played roughly half their value and with separation.

VOLUME SWELLS

Turn the volume knob down on your guitar then play the note in tab and quickly turn up your guitar volume and then turn back down creating volume swells.

Printed in Great Britain
by Amazon